Leon D. Adams'

Commonsense Book

of Wine

Leon D. Adams' Commonsense Book of WINE

THIRD EDITION, REVISED AND EXPANDED

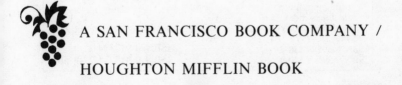

A SAN FRANCISCO BOOK COMPANY /

HOUGHTON MIFFLIN BOOK

Houghton Mifflin Company 1975 Boston

To Eleanor

C 10 9 8 7 6 5 4 3 2 1

Copyright © 1958, 1964, 1975 by Leon D. Adams

Printed in the United States of America.

This SAN FRANCISCO BOOK COMPANY/HOUGHTON MIFFLIN BOOK originated in San Francisco and was produced and published jointly. Distribution is by Houghton Mifflin Company, 2 Park Street, Boston, Massachusetts 02107.

Library of Congress Cataloging in Publication Data
Adams, Leon David, 1905–
   Leon D. Adams' Commonsense book of wine.

   "A San Francisco Book Company/Houghton Mifflin book."
   Bibliography: p.
   Includes index.
   1. Wine and wine making.   I. Title: Commonsense book of wine.
TP548.A22   1975   641.2'2   75-6805
ISBN 0-395-20438-0   **ISBN 0-913374-21-0**
ISBN 0-395-20540-9 pbk.   **ISBN 0-913374-22-9 pbk.**

Drawings by LINDA BENNETT

Contents

peramental Farm Product — Unpronounceable
Grapes — The Wine You Liked in Europe — How
Do They Really Taste?

Test — The Bordeaux Scandal — Are Women Better
Tasters? — How Does "Finesse" Taste?

Preventive of Alcoholism — Wine and the Family
— For a Maturing America

ILLUSTRATIONS

Foreword

The more wine books that are published, the more need there is for one to make sense out of the rest. The first edition of this book, published in 1958 and slightly updated in 1964, partly fulfilled that need.

But since then, wine use in this country has more than doubled, and many Americans' tastes in wine have matured. At least a hundred more books have been written in praise and explanation of this ancient, honored beverage—most of them delightful reading, but without an explanation of their explanations.

Meanwhile, the market is flooded with new wines from many countries, with labels and prices that mostly defy explanation. Moreover, many wines have changed in taste, sometimes, but not always, for the better.

Millions of Americans in homes, stores, and restaurants are asking questions about wine to which they still are unable to get understandable answers. This revised, expanded edition is addressed especially to them. Vintners will forgive me, I hope, for thereby revealing some of their well-kept secrets and for my new, somewhat arbitrary attempt to classify their products by taste. My purpose, as in the earlier editions, is to supply some much-needed common sense on the delicious subject of wine.

Leon D. Adams

Sausalito, California
February 1975

1 / How to Be a Wine Connoisseur

If you would enjoy fame as a wine expert, there is an easy way to acquire that reputation.

Next time you are served a glass of wine, lift it by the stem (not the bowl!). Wave it under your nose with a circular motion. Smell the wine, and look thoughtful. Take a sip, cautiously. Then, find fault with it. This is the sure-fire way to have others regard you as a connoisseur. Although it will get you by (it always works when I use it), you will only have qualified, thus far, as a wine snob.

If, on the other hand, you genuinely wish to cure your awe of unpronounceable wine labels, to hold your own in a wine discussion, to avoid being fleeced by nasty waiters, and to enjoy this delightful beverage within your budget and without the risk of committing social hara-kiri, read on. These pages will unravel for you most of the mystery that enshrouds the thousands of different nectars fermented from grapes. The flavors, colors, uses, alcoholic strengths, and pricing of wines will be explained. You will know how to taste, buy, serve, and care for them, how to appreciate them, and how not to be a wine snob.

What is wine snobbery? Who are the connoisseurs? What makes one a wine expert?

A genuine wine expert is one who can readily distinguish among the world's principal wines without seeing the labels. The number of such people is surprisingly few. You can become one, if your senses of taste and smell are normally keen, by sampling a sufficient number of wines with an open mind and retentive memory, and by learning at the same time about the principal wine grape varieties and how simply wines are made.

To be a wine connoisseur, it is not necessary to be such an expert. Surely you are already a connoisseur (which means a critical judge) of steaks, roasts, coffee, catsup, and also perhaps of Bourbon, Scotch, or cigarettes. In fact, we are all connoisseurs of the things we especially enjoy in food, drink, and entertainment. We are not shy about discussing our likes and dislikes among such things. Why be shy about discussing our likes and dislikes among wines? Your taste is unique just as your thumb print is. You alone are the judge of what pleases your discriminating eye, nose, and palate. You are a connoisseur of wines when you have sampled enough of them to know which ones please you and which do not. (My children were wine connoisseurs by the time they were twelve years of age.)

You are a wine snob, on the other hand, if (a) you look for a wine's faults instead of its virtues, if (b) you are influenced by a wine's price instead of by its flavor, if (c) you turn up your nose at bottles that lack famous names or vintage dates, or, in general, if you drink the label instead of the wine.

From the above distinctions it is readily apparent that while wine snobs are not necessarily experts or connoisseurs, you are likely to find many connoisseurs and even some experts behaving like wine snobs.

Yet there is no particular harm in wine snobbery. In fact, it is fun, and might even be recommended as an easily acquired mark of gentility. Other cultural endeavors get welcome support from art snobs, book snobs, and music snobs, to name a few kinds. All of them enjoy themselves and derive benefit therefrom. And since it is better to confess than to be exposed, I shall admit that in serving and discussing wines I occasionally practice a little snobbery myself.

Wines offer an uniquely rich opportunity for snobs to pretend they are experts. On a subject as tangled as this one, almost anybody can expound safely because hardly anyone else knows what is right or wrong. There are in the world at least a quarter of a million wines with established names, so no human being can possibly know them all. Anyone who tries to make you believe that he knows all about wines is obviously a fake.

Don't rely on such phony experts, or on anybody else who may try to tell you which wine you should or shouldn't like. When you let your own taste be your guide, you are a connoisseur.

3

2 / Why Drink It?

At dinner one evening when he was eight years old, my son Tim asked me, "What is wine, Dad?"

I answered him: "If you squeeze a handful of grapes and leave the juice in a cup, tiny yeast plants on the grape skins will turn the juice into wine." Then I continued, explaining that the yeasts change the natural grape sugar into alcohol and carbon dioxide gas, which bubbles away; that red wine gets its color from the skins, while white wine is fermented from the juice alone; that the winemaker must protect the wine from spoilage, moving it from cask to cask until it becomes clear, and that the wine must be allowed to age for months or years before it is ready to drink.

Tim's brow knit in perplexed thought while I told him all this. Then his face lit up with the bright light of sudden comprehension. "I know now what you mean, Dad!" he exclaimed. "Wine is just old grape juice."

Young Tim was right, of course, and his youthfully

simple definition best explains the nature of wine, the fruit juice that preserves itself, the wholesome natural beverage instead of water to drink with food. Naturally fermented, dry table wine, the principal kind of wine used in the world, is the only true mealtime beverage. Unlike water, coffee, tea, soft drinks, beer, or milk, it has few other uses except to accompany the main course of a meal.

It is also the only beverage that offers a complete range of the four taste elements to which the human palate is sensitive—sweetness, acidity, saltiness, and bitterness—to balance these same flavor elements in solid foods. It supplies aroma, acidity, and smoothness to foods that lack those qualities. It accents food flavors, fulfilling the function of a sauce; it is the sauce that you drink. Gourmets and authors of cookbooks praise it as an inseparable companion of fine foods. It is an indispensable ingredient of fine cookery.

Wine is much more. It is the sacred, symbolic, romantic beverage, the only one fittingly used to celebrate the holy Mass, to launch ships, to make the connoisseur's banquet perfect, to toast bride, beggar, or king. Its praises have been sung for centuries in literature and music.

The homage paid to wine is richly deserved. As the blood of the grape, bestowed by Nature with the magic power to create happiness, it has sacred religious symbolism; it even represents the blood of Christ. Its beginnings are lost in antiquity; its ancient history is traced from the hieroglyphics of Egypt and Babylon, from the writings of Greek and Roman poets, and from no less than one hundred and sixty-five references in the Bible. Philosophers and physicians have praised wine since the dawn of civilization as an adjunct to life, health, and happiness. Through all the ages of man it has been associated with feasting, philosophy, art, music, and love.

But if a vintner were to tell you, in one of his advertisements, that you should also drink wine because it is a healthful drink, he would be promptly taken to task by the United States government, which has the power to revoke his license and put him out of business. There is a federal regulation, ambiguous in its language but backed up by some unambiguous bureaucratic rulings, that effectively prevents him from advertising this fact. Since I am not a vintner and therefore hold no license for the government to revoke, I can tell you this important truth and others besides.

Before anyone asks, "Aren't beer, whisky and gin the same as wine?" and "Are you advocating that we all become alcoholics?" let me answer both questions.

Wine is a natural product; malt and distilled beverages are manufactured. There is a great deal more in wine than mere alcohol. It has been medically substantiated that wines, depending on their type, not only contain fruit sugars valuable in the diet, but in addition are the only common alcoholic beverages containing significant quantitites of the B vitamins, plus all of the thirteen mineral elements recognized as essential to maintain animal and human life. They also have the ability to improve appetite and promote digestion.

It is their nonalcoholic components, not found in

spirituous beverages, that make wines behave differently in the human body. Somehow, in ways not yet fully understood by medical researchers, the organic acids, esters, and nitrogen-bearing compounds in wines *slow down* the rate at which the alcohol in wines enters your bloodstream. This slow rate of absorption is important. Your blood-alcohol level, when you drink wine, reaches a plateau instead of a peak. The alcohol circulates at low levels through your body, where it lulls and helps to relax your jumpy nerve centers; you feel a pleasant glow. The pleasant feeling from wine lasts longer than that from other drinks. Alcohol from the others gets into your blood more quickly; its effects are more sudden and more pronounced.

In other words, don't drink wine for a "kick," because if it's a kick you want, you will get it fastest and hardest from vodka. Wine's alcoholic effect is more gradual. Or if you prefer the testimony of folklore, there's the jingle that paraphrases Ogden Nash:

> Candy's dandy
> Wine's fine
> But likker's quicker.

Some noted medical authorities have said that wine is the best of all tranquilizers and that it could well supplant 90 percent of the drugs used to induce sleep. There is reason to wonder whether Americans would be gulping a quarter-billion aspirin tablets every twenty-four hours to reduce pain (this was the rate calculated in 1972) if more people used wine. Pharmaceutical firms in Italy are reported to be unhappy because they cannot find many customers for their tranquilizers and other happy-pills in that country, where nearly everyone drinks wine instead of water.

There is plentiful medical testimony that tension, stress, or chronic anxiety is a national disease among Americans in this age of nuclear bombs and chronic inflation. I suspect that if a survey were made among people who regularly have wine with dinner or who take a glass of wine before dinner, it would show that most of them enjoy emotional comfort in the evenings, sleep well, and need no manufactured tranquilizers. As one busy mother expressed it succinctly when I interviewed her in the course of a survey I once conducted among sherry consumers, "A glass of sherry before dinner gets me past the suicide hour."

But since everyone knows that wine has been the joy of mankind for centuries, you may ask, at this point, how this beverage can make you happy when it also makes you drowsy. The answer is that it depends on the quantity consumed, the circumstances, and on your individual body chemistry at the time you drink wine. Some of us become happy, then sleepy. Others are relaxed at first, then joyful. Some stay wide-awake all evening.

Enough, however, about the tranquilizing, joy-promoting, and soporific qualities of wine, because in the chapter entitled "Is Wine for You?" I report still other interesting things doctors now know about the various alcoholic beverages, including when these should not be drunk at all.

As for wines' appetite- and digestion-promoting values, these too are taboo in vintners' advertising. The government even considers it a crime for a winery to quote the Bible passage in which Paul admonishes Timothy to "use a little wine for thy stomach's sake and thine often infirmities . . ."

Note that Paul advises "a little" wine. Too much wine, like too much whisky, too much medicine, too much salt, or even too much water, can injure or even kill.

Despite the taboos against telling the truth, wine use in America has doubled and table wine use has more than trebled since 1964. Thus far, however, this has occurred mostly in certain favored localities. You find wine always served where there is fine food. You never find it in homes or restaurants where hurried, tasteless meals are had with ice water as the beverage.

Vast areas of the United States and Canada have not as yet been subjected to the civilizing influence of flavorful cuisine. Many Prohibitionist-dominated localities in the midwestern, southern, and northern states have not yet had their tastes refined by leisurely gourmet dining and its inseparable companion, wine. In those gastronomic deserts of America, wine, which enhances food flavors, does not compete with catsup, which hides flavors that usually deserve to be hidden.

Yet there is hope for the future of gastronomy on this continent, because increasing travel to our chief winegrowing states and to the wine countries of Europe is exposing millions of Americans to the delights of civilized dining. Also, increasing leisure always starts people searching for ways to make life richer. They discover that wine is a symbol of gracious living and

9

of hospitality, and that it is also a glamorous ornament. No one thing can add as much charm to dining as wine glasses and a bottle or decanter on the table with the silver, china, and flowers—whether the guests drink the wine or not. Can you think of any other food item that inspires mealtime conversation like a fine wine on the table?

Knowledge of wines and ability to discuss them were once talents possessed by only a few well-traveled individuals. Now these talents are fast becoming widespread. The appreciation of wine is as essential a mark of culture as the appreciation of art, of music, and of literature. This is one of the reasons why my evening college classes in wine appreciation are oversubscribed before they begin.

Yet with all of its recommendations, the blood of the grape also represents economy. In most of this country, despite a burden of gallonage taxes, greater in some states than the cost of the product itself, wholesome everyday table wine is the best beverage bargain the public can buy. Purchased in thrifty jugs, now available everywhere, it costs pennies a glass, one of the less expensive yet most flavorful ingredients of a fine meal.

Why drink wine? Ernest Hemingway may have answered that question best when he wrote:

Wine is one of the most civilized things in the world and one of the natural things of the world that has been brought to the greatest perfection; and it offers a greater range for enjoyment and appreciation than possibly any other purely sensory thing which may be purchased.

3 / Wines Unraveled

The most confusing thing about wines is their nomenclature, their thousands of different names and descriptive legends that bewilder the wine-buying public, wine-store personnel, restaurateurs, and even many of the vintners themselves.

Granted, this is a delicious kind of confusion, and the complexity of wines is part of their charm. But the nomenclature tangle is multiplying beyond normal comprehension as our vintners and importers continue introducing more and more wines with strange names.

This presents a challenge to those of us who teach professionally about wine, and particularly to me, because I once undertook the Augean project of directing the education of Americans in the understanding and appreciation of wine. Much of my labor during my twenty years at the Wine Institute was in trying to make sense out of wine names. That effort even led me many years ago to write *The Wine Study Course,* first published in 1943. I slashed through the world's wine lists and arbitrarily reduced all the kinds to five main classes according to use: "appetizer," "white table," "red (and pink) table," "dessert," and "sparkling." These simplified many restaurant wine lists and eventually achieved legal status in government regulations.

More than a half million people in a dozen countries have since studied the *Wine Study Course* texts, passed the written examinations and received their diplomas as graduates. The industry's advertisements, booklets, and leaflets by the billions have saturated the nation, attempting thus to simplify wine. But the confusion grows. My "five classes" have helped to teach the uses of wine, but as an attempt to unscramble the crazy quilt of names, they have failed.

I therefore now teach a different method of classifying wines—by taste, color, and alcoholic strength. It makes sense, because every wine is either dry, medium-dry, or sweet; every wine is either red, pink, amber, or white; and every wine is either still, semi-bubbly, or sparkling. Moreover, virtually all wines either contain 9 to 12 percent alcohol or else fit into the 17 to 20 percent group. There also are a few easily recognizable flavors that can be named.

This classification has made sense in the earlier editions of this book and to my students in the classes I have taught in recent years. (I do not attempt to cover the countless wines made of fruits other than grapes. They usually have the flavors of the fruits named and are mostly low in alcoholic content, and sweet.)

In the earlier editions, this chapter classified into flavor groups the 181 wine names then often found on wine bottles in stores and restaurants in the United States. The list has since grown to 362. You will find it in a separate section, beginning on page 20, entitled "Key to 362 Wines."

The Key tells you, insofar as possible, what a wine's name rarely tells: how that particular wine is likely to taste if you open the bottle and pour yourself a glass. I emphasize *insofar as possible* because wines change in taste from year to year without changing their labels—a form of vintners' license that endlessly baffles their customers. Another reason is that—as you will see in the Key—many single wine names are used to represent two or more quite different tasting or different colored wines. The 362 names in the Key actually represent 546 different wines.

In the Key to wine colors "white" means wines that are either straw-colored, golden, or light amber. "Amber" refers to wines of oxidized character, which range from palest amber to the darkest brown. "Red" wines vary from light garnet and tawny to deep ruby. The alcoholic-content figures represent only averages for the products most widely sold; individual wines vary a few degrees in strength.

"Dry" as used in the Key means what it does in your dictionary—without sweetness—the exact opposite of "sweet." This is not what "dry" means on many wine labels, however, because many vintners—unwilling to call their wines sweet because they believe it would impede their sales—make them partially sweet but label them "dry." Such wines are identified in the Key as "medium dry," by which I mean the taste you

13

get from one lump of sugar in your coffee. "Medium sweet" in the Key would represent a second or third lump, "sweet" a fourth or fifth. (I am describing sweet *taste,* not sugar content as wine chemists measure it, which is quite a different matter.)

"Tart" describes the fresh, fruit-acid taste of most dry wines; without tartness they would taste flat. "Astringent," which many dry red wines are, means puckery from their tannin content, the same mouth sensation you get from overly strong tea. Really dry, tart, astringent red wines are not ordinarily liked by beginners at first taste. You get to like these after repeated use, the way you gradually acquire a taste for strong cheeses, green olives, or black, unsweetened coffee. Such wines best match the high flavors of hearty foods. "Soft" in the Key refers to red wines that are *not* astringent.

"Varietal" identifies wines named for the grape varieties from which they are predominantly made. "Labrusca" means the pronounced grapy flavor you taste in bottled or canned grape juice and in grape jelly. It is the "foxy" personality of the Concord grape variety and its many relatives. Labrusca is the viticulturist's name for this particular family of wild, now domesticated, American vines. "Spicy" refers to wines with pronounced varietal aroma and taste, such as those of Gewürztraminer, Sauvignon Blanc, and the Muscadine native grape family of the southeastern states, whose wines are mostly sold as Scuppernong.

It is probably a form of Bacchic blasphemy to treat

14

wine, the most honored of beverages, as merely another drink. Yet soda pop—in contrast to the blood of the grape—comes in only about twenty most popular flavors. Beer has five, more or less; whisky perhaps eight; and the dairy industry now offers us, as beverages, homogenized milk, condensed, evaporated, and powdered milks, buttermilk, skim milk, chocolate milk, and for folks with certain allergies, goat's milk. Why not describe wines, too, according to their usual flavors?

To this question vintners usually reply that the products of the world's myriad vineyards cannot be described as simply as the manufactured uniform flavors of soft drinks. They point out that wines are farm products, as temperamental as the local weather that influences the flavors of their grapes, just as it influences the taste of apples, plums, peaches, and other fruits and vegetables from season to season. This is why Europeans are content to name their wines for the thousands of geographic localities where they are grown, most of which cannot be found on their countries' maps. Now we have the scores of new varietal labels, which name wines for their sometimes unpronounceable grape varieties. Varietally-named wines vary in taste because winemakers' flavor preferences and methods differ, and because the same grape variety grown in different localities produces different, often markedly different, wines.

There are a few world-traveled experts who know the intricate local geography of many grape-growing regions, and some who possess some knowledge of

15

grape ampelography. But to the uninformed, untraveled buyer, geographic and varietal names are mostly euphonious gibberish.

Vintners will surely disagree with the helter-skelter way in which I have arbitrarily given their costliest, finest, aged vintages the same broad flavor descriptions as the youngest, least expensive wines of similar types. For that matter, vintners do not agree on wine-name meanings among themselves. Let me illustrate with a bit of history.

Some years ago the staff of the Wine Institute, appalled by the confusion then existing, undertook to prepare a set of definitions of the principal California wine types and to write them into a state regulation to guide producers, merchants, and beverage-control officials. The importance of the undertaking can be appreciated when one remembers that California supplies roughly three fourths of all the wine consumed in the United States.

Our staff research into European laws and regulations cast no light. In Europe, elaborate laws mainly define the thousands of little viticultural districts but fail to specify how a wine under a given name shall taste.

We then quizzed California vintners, individually and at industry meetings, on what their labels meant. We soon learned that one winery's sauterne matched another winery's haut sauterne; that John Doe's "regular" sherry was drier than Richard Roe's "dry" sherry; and so on through the entire list of popular types.

Using more wheedling than logic, we finally won

most wineries' agreement to let us spell out measurable steps of sweetness for "dry," "regular," "haut" (sweet), and "château" (still sweeter) sauternes, and for "dry," "regular," and sweet ("cream," "golden," or "mellow") sherries.

The day arrived for the official State of California hearing on the proposed regulations. Before the time came to discuss sauternes, the spokesman for a group of wineries made an announcement. "We are artists," he said. "We cannot agree to make our wines all the same. We oppose any definition for sauternes."

Unable to answer that one, we contented ourselves with offering regulative definitions of the three not-too-rigid sweetness levels for sherries. These scraped through the hearing with only minor opposition. (By these regulations, California dry sherry may not be over 2.5 grams in sweetness; "sherry" without a dryness label must be between 2.5 and 4.0 grams, and if labeled "sweet" or with its synonyms must be over 4.0 grams "in reducing sugar content per 100 milliters at 20° Centigrade and calculated as dextrose." Sweet dessert wines are regulated differently, by the Brix saccharometer test. These California wines are required to test not less than 5.5 degrees Brix for angelica, muscatel, and ports, and not less than 3.5 for tokay.)

If you ever have occasion to read the California regulations—which I am not recommending for entertainment—please remember that confusing though they are, no other wine regulations in the world give nearly as much flavor information as these do.

My flavor Key gives you at least a preliminary idea

of how a wine is likely to taste. I will even go a step farther and venture that if you have already found you enjoy a wine type roughly described, there is a reasonable possibility you will also like most of the others with the same description. This also may answer the question often asked by those who return from trips abroad: "Where can I find an American wine like the one I enjoyed in Europe?" The Meursault or chablis you liked in France has reasonable counterparts in its American relatives, Chardonnay and Pinot Blanc. If a famous red Bordeaux has pleased you, so will many well-made Cabernet Sauvignons of equal age; and so on.

Since this book was first published, there has been a marked improvement in the amount of information given on wine labels. Some European bottles supply basic helpful information, usually on added strip-labels, but in very small type that you have to strain to read, such as "white table wine," "red Bordeaux wine," and "semi-dry white Vouvray wine." American vintners have been the leaders in this trend, especially with labels giving advice about wine-serving temperatures and foods with which their wines harmonize best. Some back-labels now offer more information than the buyer has time to read.

My Key to 362 Wines, however, does not recommend any specific wines for you, because each of us finds his personal choice among wines, as he does among friends, sweethearts, newspapers, magazines, music, or automobiles. I have attempted only to unravel the bare designations that imply flavors, colors, and alcoholic

18

strength. The strange meanings of some other words and symbols that you see displayed on bottles are explained in a later chapter entitled "Some Labels Unriddled," and others will be found in the Glossary. .

KEY TO 362 WINES

Here are the 362 wine names most often found on bottle labels in stores and restaurant wine lists in the United States and Canada. The Key tells you each wine's color (white, amber, pink, red); its flavor (degree of dryness or sweetness); whether it is tart, astringent, soft, spicy, oxidized, bubbly or sparkling); whether its name is varietal (named for a grape); its approximate alcoholic strength; and how its name is pronounced.

Wines produced only in specific localities are also identified by region, such as Bordeaux (Bord), Burgundy (Burg), California (Cal), France (Fr), Germany (Ger), Hungary (Hung), Italy (Ital), the Italian Piedmont (Pied), and Portugal (Por). Wines not so identified have generic or varietal names and can be produced anywhere.

LEGEND

bubbly—semi-sparkling	ox—oxidized like sherry
dry—without sweetness	soft—not astringent
dry red—dry, tart, astringent (puckery)	spicy—pronounced varietal aroma, taste
dry white—dry, tart	spk—sparkling
flav—flavored	*see*—refer to Glossary or Index
Lab—Labrusca (grapy, foxy)	
med-dry—medium-dry	var—varietal
med-swt—medium sweet	17–20—alcoholic strength; all others are 9 to 14%
Musc—Muscat flavor	

Affenthaler (*ah*-fen-ta-ler) dry red, Ger

Aglianico (ahl-*yan*-e-co) dry red, Ital

Aleatico (al-e-*ah*-te-co) sweet Musc pink and red, var

Aligoté (ah-le-go-*tay*) dry white, var

Aloxe-Corton (ahl-*ohs*-cor-*tohn*) dry soft red and dry white, Burg

Amontillado (ah-mohn-te-*yah*-do) dry ox amber, 17–20, *see*

Amoroso sweet ox amber, 17–20, *see*

Angelica sweet white, Cal, 18–20

Anjou (ahn-zhoo) dry and med-dry white, Fr

Arbois (ahr-bwa) dry pink, red, white, Fr

Assmanshausen (ahs-mans-how-zen) dry and med-swt red, Ger

Asti Spumante (ahs-te-spu-mahn-tay) spk med-swt Musc white, var, Pied

Auxerrois (oh-zher-wah) dry white, var, Fr

Auxey-Duresses (o-say-du-ress) dry white and soft red, Burg

Ayl (ile) dry white, Ger

Baco Noir (ba-co-nwar) dry red, hybrid var

Banyuls sweet ox white, Fr, 15–20

Barbaresco dry red, Pied

Barbera (bar-*bair*-a) dry red, var

Barberone (bar-bair-*oh*-nay) dry red

Bardolino (bar-do-*le*-no) dry soft red, Ital

Barolo dry red, Pied

Baroque proprietary dry red, Cal

Barsac (bar-sac) sweet white, Bord

Bâtard-Montrachet (*ba*-tar-mohn-rash-*ay*) dry white, Burg

Beaujolais (bo-zho-lay) dry red, some dry white, Burg

Beaune (bone) dry soft red and dry white, Burg

Beerenauslese (beer-en-ows-lay-zeh) sweet white, Ger

Bergerac (ber-zhair-ac) dry red, dry and sweet white, Fr

Bergheimer dry white; Ger

Bernkasteler dry and med-dry white, Moselle

Bingener dry and med-dry white, Ger

Black Muscat sweet Musc red, var, 18–20

Blagny (blan-ye) dry soft red, dry white, Burg

Blanc de Blancs dry to med-dry white, *see*

Blanc Fumé (blahn-foo-may) spicy dry and med-dry white, var, *see*

Blanchots (blahn-sho) dry white, Burg

Blaye (bly) dry and soft dry red, dry and med-dry white, Bord

Bodenheimer dry white, Ger

Bonnes Mares (bon-*mar*) dry soft red, Burg

Bordeaux Blanc, Rouge dry white, dry red, Fr

Borgoña dry red, Spain

Bougros (boo-gro) dry white, Burg

Bourg (boorg) dry red, med-dry white, Bord

Bourgeais (boor-zhay) dry red, med-dry white, Bord

Bourgogne (boor-gohn-yuh) dry soft red, dry red, also spk, Burg

Bourgueil (boor-guhy) dry red, Loire

Brachetto (bra-keh-to) bubbly sweet red, var, Pied

Brauneberger dry and med-dry white, Ger

Brouilly (broo-ye) dry red, Burg

Brown Sherry dry and med-dry ox, amber

Bual (boo-ahl) med-swt ox amber, var, Madeira, 17–20

Burgundy dry soft red, med-dry red, dry white

Cabernet (cab-er-*nay*) dry red and pink, var, *see*

Cahors (cah-*or*) dry red, Fr

Cairanne (cay-*rahn*) dry red, pink, white, Rhone

Carema (ca-*ray*-ma) dry red, Pied

Carignane (ca-re-*nyahn*) dry red, var

Carnelian dry red, var, Cal

Cascade dry red, hybrid var

Castelli di Jesi (dee-jez-see) dry white, Ital

Castelli Romani dry red, dry white, Ital

Catawba sweet white, sweet pink, Lab, also spk, var

Cérons (say-rohn) med-dry white, Bord

Chablis dry white, *see*

Chambertin (*shahm*-bair-tan) dry soft red, Burg

Chambolle-Musigny (chahm-bohl-mooseen-ye) dry soft red and dry white, Burg

Champagne spk dry, med-dry, and sweet, white, pink, and red

Champigny (shahm-peen-yee) dry red, Loire

Chancellor dry red, hybrid var

Charbono dry red, var

Chardonnay dry white, var

Chassagne-Montrachet (shah-*sanya*-mohn-rash-*ay*) dry soft red and dry white, Burg

Château La Salle proprietary med-dry Musc white, Cal

Châteauneuf-du-Pape (sha-to-nuf-dew-*pahp*) dry red and white, Rhone

"Château" Sauterne sweet white

Chelois (shell-wah) dry red, hybrid var

Chénas (shay-na) dry red, Burg

Chenin Blanc (shay-nan-blahn) dry or med-dry white, var

Chianti (kee-*an*-tee) dry red and white, Ital

Chiaretto (key-ar-eh-to) dry pink, Ital

Chinon (she-noh) dry red, Loire

Chiroubles (shee-rubl) dry red, Burg

Clairette dry white, also spk, var, Fr

Claret dry red

Clarete (cla-*ray*-tay) dry red, Spain

Clos de Vougeot (clo-duh-voo-zho) dry soft red and dry white, Burg

Cocktail Sherry dry to med-dry ox amber, 17–20

Colares (co-*la*-rays) dry red, Por

Cold Duck spk med-swt pink or red, some Lab

Condrieu (cohn-dree-uh) dry or med-dry white, some bubbly, Rhone

Constantia sweet Musc white, 17–20, S. Africa

Corbières (cor-be-*air*) dry red, some dry pink, white, Fr

Cornas (cor-nahs) dry red, Rhone

Corton dry soft red, also dry white, Burg

Coteaux du Layon (cot-oh-dew-lay-ohn) med-dry white, Loire

Coteaux du Languedoc (*lahng*-doc) med-dry white and dry red, Fr

Côte de Nuits (coat-duh-nwee) dry red, Burg

Côte Rôtie (coat-ro-tee) dry red, Rhone

Côtes de Bourg *see* Bourg

Côtes du Rhone dry red, some dry pink, white

Crackling Rosé bubbly med-dry pink

Cream Sherry sweet ox amber, 17–20

Cröver *see* Kröver

Dão (dawn) dry red, some dry white, Port

Deidesheimer dry or med-dry white, Ger

Delaware dry white, Lab, var

Dézaley (day-za-lay) dry white, Swiss

Diamond dry or med-dry white, Lab, var

Dolcetto (dol-*chet*-to) dry soft red, var, Pied

Dry Muscat *see* Light Dry Muscat

Dry Sack med-dry ox amber, 17–20

Dry Sauterne dry or med-dry white

Dry Sherry med-dry ox amber, 17–20

Dubonnet proprietary flav sweet red, 17–20
Dutchess dry or med-dry white, Lab, var

Échézeaux (esh-ay-zo) dry soft red, Burg
Edelzwicker dry white, Alsace
Egri Bikaver (eg-ree-be-ka-vair) dry red, Hung
Eiswein sweet white, Ger, *see*
Eitelsbacher dry or med-dry white, Moselle
Eltviller dry or med-dry white, Ger
Elvira dry or med-dry white, Lab, var
Emerald Riesling dry or med-dry white, var
Entre-deux-Mers (on-truh-duh-mair) dry white, Bord
Erbacher dry and med-dry white, Ger
Est! Est! Est! med-dry white, Ital
Extra Dry Champagne spk med-dry white
Faverges (fa-vairzh) dry white, Swiss
Fendant (fawn-don) dry white, var, Swiss
Fino Sherry dry ox amber, Spain, 17–20
Fitou (fee-too) dry red, Fr
Fixin (feex-an) dry soft red, Burg
Flagey (fla-zhay) dry soft red, Burg
Fleurie (flur-ree) dry red, Burg
Flora spicy dry or med-dry white, var
Flor Sherry dry or med-dry ox amber, 17–20
Foch (fohsh) dry red, hybrid var
Folle Blanche (foal-blahnsh) dry white, var
Forster dry or med-dry white, Ger
Fourchaume (foor-shome) dry white, Burg
Franken Riesling dry or med-dry white, var, *see*
Frascati dry white, Ital
Frecciarossa (fretch-a-rohs-sa) dry red, pink, white, proprie-
   tary Ital
Freisa (*fray*-sa) dry or med-dry red, some bubbly, var

25

French Colombard dry white, var
French Vermouth flav dry amber, 17–20
Fumé Blanc (foo-may-blahn) dry and med-dry white, var,
    see

Gamay dry red and pink, var, *see*
Gamay Beaujolais dry red, var, *see*
Gamay Noir dry red, var, *see*
Gattinara (ga-tee-*na*-ra) dry red, Pied
Geisenheimer dry white, Ger
Ghemme dry red, Ital
Gevrey-Chambertin (zhev-ray-shahm-bair-tan) dry soft red,
    Burg
Gewürztraminer (ge-vertz-tram-me-ner) spicy dry or med-dry
    white, var
Gigondas (zhe-gon-das) dry soft red, also dry pink, Rhone
Givry (zhe-vree) dry red and white, Burg
Graacher dry and med-dry white, Moselle
Graves (grahv) dry red and white, Bord
Green Hungarian med-dry white, var
Grenache (gren-nahsh) dry and med-dry pink and dry red,
    var
Grey Riesling dry white, var
Grignolino (gree-nyo-lee-no) dry pink and dry soft red, var
Grinzinger dry and med-dry white, Austria
Grumello dry red, Ital
Gumpoldskirchener (goom-polds-keerk-ener) dry white,
    Austria
Gutedel (goot-eh-del) dry white, var

Haut-Médoc (oh-may-doc) dry red, Bord
Haut Sauterne (oh-so-tairn) sweet white
Hermitage (air-me-tazh) dry red, dry and med-dry white,
    Rhone

Hochheimer dry and med-dry white, Ger
Hock dry and med-dry white
Hospices de Beaune (os-peace-duh-bone) dry soft red and
   dry white, Burg

Isabella Rosé med-dry pink Lab, var
Italian Vermouth flav sweet red, 16–20
Ives dry and med-dry red Lab, var

Jesuitengarten (yez-u-eet-en-garten) med-dry and sweet
   white, Ger
Johannisberger dry and med-dry white, Ger
Johannisberg Riesling dry and med-dry white, var
Juliénas (jul-yea-na) dry red, Burg
Jurançon (zhoo-ran-sohn) dry and sweet white, Fr

Kiedricher dry and med-dry white, Ger
Kokineli flav sweet pink
Kosher dry, med-dry, and sweet types, but mainly sweet
   Lab
Kreuznacher (kroytz-nacher) dry and med-dry white, Ger
Kröver dry and med-dry white, Moselle

Lacrima Christi dry or sweet white, pink, and red, also spk,
   Ital
Lacrima d'Arno dry white, Ital
Lafões (la-foish) dry red or white, usually bubbly, Por
Lambrusco bubbly med-dry to med-swt red, var, Ital
Laubenheimer dry and med-dry white, Ger
Liebfraumilch (leeb-frow-milsh) dry and med-dry white, also
   spk, Ger
Light Dry Muscat med-dry Musc white, var
Lillet flav med-dry amber, 17–20, Fr

Listrac dry red, Bord
Loupiac sweet white, Bord

Macon (mac-cohn) dry and med-dry red, pink, white, Burg
Madeira dry, med-dry, and sweet ox amber, 17–20
Malaga sweet red, 17–20, some Lab 9–12
Malbec dry red, var
Malmsey med-swt ox amber, var, Madeira, 17–20
Malvasia Bianca med-dry Musc white, var
Malvoisie (mal-vwa-zee) sweet ox amber, var, 17–20
Manzanilla (mahn-tha-neel-ya) dry and med-dry ox amber, Spain, 17–20
Marcobrunner dry to med-swt white, Ger
Margaux (mar-go) dry red, Bord
Marsala dry to sweet ox amber, also flav, 17–20
Mateus (ma-tay-oosh) proprietary bubbly med-dry pink, Por
Mavrodaphne sweet, red, Greece, 16–20
May Wine flav med-dry white
Médoc (may-doc) dry red, Bord
Mercurey (mer-coo-ray) dry red, some dry white, Burg
Merlot (mer-lo) dry red, var
Meursault (mur-so) dry white, Burg
Minervois (me-nair-vwah) dry red, Fr
Monbazillac (mohn-baz-e-yac) sweet white, Fr
Montilla (mon-*tee*-ya) dry to med-dry ox amber, Spain, 15–16
Montlouis (mohn-loo-we) dry and med-dry white, some spk, Loire
Montrachet (mohn-rah-shay) dry white, Burg
Moore's Diamond dry or med-dry white, Lab, var
Morgon (mor-gohn) dry red, Burg
Moscato Amabile (mos-*cah*-to ah-*mah*-bee-lay) med-dry to sweet Musc white, var, some spk

Moscato Canelli med-swt Musc white, var
Moselblümchen med-dry white, Moselle
Moselle, Mosel dry and med-dry white
Moulin-á-Vent (moo-lan-a-von) dry red, Burg
Moulis (moo-lee) dry red, Bord
Muscadelle du Bordelais med-dry white, var
Muscadet (mus-ca-day) dry white, Loire
Muscadine spicy sweet red, pink, white, var, *see*
Muscat med-dry to sweet Musc white, var
Muscatel sweet Musc white, var, 18–20
Muscat Frontignan white sweet Musc, var, 17–20
Muscat Ottonel med-dry Musc white, var
Musigny (moo-seen-ye) dry soft red, some dry white, Burg

Nahe (*na*-huh) dry to med-dry white, Ger
Nebbiolo dry red, also sweet spk, var
Neuchâtel dry and med-dry white, some bubbly, Swiss
Niagara dry and med-dry white, Lab, var
Niersteiner dry and med-dry white, Ger
Noah dry and med-dry red, Lab, var
Nuits-St. Georges (nwee-san-zhorzh) dry soft red, some dry white, Burg

Ockfener dry and med-dry white, Ger
Oloroso Sherry dry to med-swt ox amber, Spain, 17–20
Oppenheimer dry to med-dry white, Ger
Orvieto (or-ve-eh-to) dry to sweet white, some pink, Ital

Panadés (pan-ah-*dess*) dry, sweet and spk red and white, Spain
Pauillac (po-yac) dry red, Bord
Pernand-Vergelesses (per-nahn-vair-juh-less) dry red and white, Burg

Petite Sirah (puh-teet see-rah) dry red, dry and med-dry pink, var

Piesporter dry and med-dry white, Moselle

Pinard (pee-nar) dry red

Pineau de la Loire (pee-no-duh-la-lwar) dry and med-dry white, var, *see*

Pineau des Charentes (pee-no day-sha-ront) sweet white, Fr, 18–20

Pinotage (pee-no-tahzh) dry red, var

Pinot Blanc (pee-no blahn) dry white, var

Pinot Chardonnay *see* Chardonnay

Pinot Grigio (greej-yo) dry white, var, Ital

Pinot Noir (pee-no nwahr) dry red, var

Pinot Rosé dry pink, var

Pinot St. George dry red, var

Pomerol dry red, Bord

Pommard (po-mar) dry soft red, Burg

Port, Porto sweet red, 18–20

Pouilly-Fuissé (poo-yee-fwee-say) dry white, Burg

Pouilly-Fumé (few-may) dry and med-dry white, Loire

Pouilly-sur-Loire dry and med-dry white, Fr

Preuses (pruhz) dry white, Burg

Puligny-Montrachet (poo-leen-ye-mohn-rash-ay) dry white, Burg

Raboso del Piave dry red, var

Rainwater med swt ox amber, Madeira, 17–20

Raphaël proprietary flav sweet red, Fr

Rauenthaler (rau-en-ta-ler) dry to med-swt white, Ger

Recioto (reh-cheo-to) sweet red, some bubbly, Ital

Red Muscatel sweet Musc red, var, 18–20

Red Pinot dry red, var

Refosco dry red, var

Retsina flav med-dry white, *see*

Richebourg (reesh-boorg) dry soft red, Burg

Riesling, Rizling dry to med-dry white, var

Rheingau dry to med-swt white, Ger

Rheinhessen dry to med-swt white, Ger

Rheinpfalz dry to med-swt white, Ger

Rhine, Rhein, Rhin dry to med-dry white

Rhine (American, New York, Ohio, etc.) dry and med-dry white, usually Lab

Rioja (ree-*oh*-ha) dry red and white, Spain

Romanée (roman-ay) dry soft red, Burg

Rosé dry to sweet pink

Rubion proprietary dry red, Cal

Ruby Cabernet dry red, var

Rüdesheimer dry and medium-dry white, Ger

Rully (roo-ye) dry red and white, some red spk, Burg

Sainte-Croix-du-Mont (sant-crwa-dew-mohn) sweet white, Fr

Saint-Emilion dry red, Bord

Saint-Estephe dry red, Bord

Saint-Julien dry red, Bordeaux

Saint-Véran (sant-vay-ron) dry white, Burg

Sancerre (sahn-sair) spicy dry white, some dry pink and red, Loire

Sangre de Toro (san-gray-day-toro) dry red, Spain

Sangría flav sweet red and white, some bubbly

St. Helena dry white, Greece

St. Raphaël *see* Raphaël

Santenay dry red and white, Burg

Sassella dry red, Ital

Saumur (so-muhr) dry and med-dry white and spk, Loire

Sauterne, Sauternes (so-tairn) sweet white, some dry or med-dry

31

Sauvignon Blanc (so-veen-yohn blanh) spicy white, var, *see*
Savigny-les-Beaune (sav-een-ye-lay-bone) dry red, some dry
  white, Burg
Scuppernong spicy, med-dry and sweet white, var, *see*
Sémillon (sem-ee-yohn) dry to sweet white, var
Sercial (sair-syal) dry ox amber, var, Madeira, 17–20
Seyval Blanc (say-val blahn) dry and med-dry white, hybrid
  var
Sherry dry to sweet ox amber, 17–20
Soave (swa-vay) dry white, Ital
Solera (so-*lay*-ra) **Sherry** dry to med-swt ox amber, 17–20
Spañada proprietary flav sweet pink, bubbly
Sparkling Burgundy spk med-dry red
Sparkling Moselle spk dry to sweet white
Sparkling Muscat spk med-dry to sweet Musc white, var
Sparkling Rosé spk dry to med-dry pink
Steinberger dry to med-swt white, Ger
Steinwein dry white, Ger
Sylvaner (sil-*vah*-ner) dry white, var

Tavel (ta-*vel*) dry pink, Rhone
Tawny Port red sweet, 18–20
Tokaj, Tokaji (to-*kye*) sweet and dry white, Hung
Tokay (California) med-swt pink or amber, 18–20
Tokay d'Alsace dry white, Alsace
Traminer (tra-mee-ner) dry white, var
Trebbiano (treb-ya-no) dry white, var
Trittenheimer dry white, Moselle

Uerziger (ert-zig-er) dry to med-dry, Moselle
Ugni Blanc (oon-ye-blahn) dry to med-dry white, var

Vaillons (vye-yohn) dry white, Burg
Valais (val-ay) dry red and white, Swiss

32

Valpolicella (val-po-lee-chel-la) dry soft red, Ital
Valtellina dry red, Ital
Vaudésir (vo-day-zeer) dry white, Burg
Verdelho (ver-del-yo) dry ox amber, var, Madeira, 17-20
Verdicchio (ver-deek-yo) dry white, Ital
Vermouth flav dry to sweet white and red, 16-20
Vinho Verde (veen-yo-vair-day) bubbly dry red and white, Por
Vino dry to med-swt soft red and white
Vin Santo (veen-santo) white and red sweet, Ital
Volnay dry soft red, Burg
Vosnes-Romanée (vohn-ro-ma-nay) dry soft red, Burg
Vougeot (voo-zho) dry soft red, Burg
Vouvray dry to med-dry white, some spk, Loire

Wallufer (vah-*loof*-er) dry to med-dry white, some dry red, Ger
Wehlener (*vay*-len-er) dry to med-dry white, Moselle
White Burgundy dry white
White Chianti dry white
White Pinot dry white, var
White Riesling dry to med-dry white, var, *see*
Wiltinger (vil-ting-er) dry to med-dry white, Ger
Winkeler (vink-ler) dry to med-dry white, Ger
Wintricher (vin-trish-er) dry to med-dry white, Moselle
Würzburger (voortz-burger) dry white, Ger

Zeller (tseller) dry white, Moselle
Zeltinger (tsel-tinger) dry to med-dry white, Moselle
Zinfandel dry red, dry pink, few dry white, var
Zwicker (zvick-er) dry white, Alsace

33

4 / Wine Shoppers' Secrets

The majority of wine producers and importers who chance to read this chapter are likely to disapprove of its blunt language. It is an attempt to help you select wines that will fit your taste, purse, and purpose.

Thousands of people are continually asking those of us who are supposed to know: "What wine shall I buy?" Sometimes the questioner adds, with a note of despair: "Never mind giving me a lecture; just tell me the name of the wine and where I can buy it." If I could answer the question simply, I would.

I can name for you, on the day this paragraph is written, a number of wines that are likely to please you and your guests, if you buy them right now in the San Francisco Bay Area. By the time you read this, my advice will be out of date. It would not guide you soundly, anyhow, in Pittsburgh, Bangor, Indianapolis, or Los Angeles. Some of the finest wines can be bought in only a few parts of the United States.

Most other wine books rate and recommend individual vintners' wines by brands and types. Wine columnists and writers of "consumer wineletters" have won wide followings in several cities by reporting on the wines they taste and by guiding their readers to what they consider "best buys," with which I sometimes agree. I am stating why this book does not recommend wines by brand. Wines, unlike other processed foods, are constantly changing, not only from vintage to vintage, but from month to month in their casks, often making it necessary for vintners to change their blends. Moreover, wines continue to change in the bottle, especially when they travel and while they stand in the store. This variability is one of the reasons wine is such a fascinating topic of discussion. It is also one of the reasons why the next few pages, which contain some secrets known to hardened wine shoppers, may make your wine buying easier.

TO FIND WHAT YOU LIKE

If you are not now a wine buyer, and are about to get your feet wet for the first time, it is pertinent to note that nobody ever learned to swim from a textbook. The only way to decide whether you will like or dislike rutabaga, endive, watercress, or other unfamiliar vegetables is to taste them. Likewise, to find which wine flavors please you, you have to taste enough different kinds.

Don't give up too easily, because it has been proved conclusively, by taste tests administered to thousands of people, that somewhere in the wonderfully wide flavor spectrum of wines there are always one or more nectars to delight each individual's taste.

The best and least expensive way to sample many wines (handy for experienced shoppers, too) is to visit the wineries that offer tasting for their visitors. There are hundreds of such wineries in the United States, more than a hundred in California alone. You probably also get occasional invitations to group wine-tastings, the instructive kind of social event that clubs and churches sponsor nowadays for their members and friends because they find it more temperate and less costly than cocktail parties.

If your neighborhood does not offer these pleasant sampling opportunities, perhaps some kind friend will serve you a wine that you discover you especially like (in which case be sure to copy the label and learn exactly where he bought it). Otherwise you will have to pay your way in the tasting department.

Ordinarily this means investing a few dollars in pure shopping adventure. It involves buying different types and brands more or less at random from the vast array on store shelves, taking them home and sampling them.

Why not invite a few friends to share the expense and the fun of a do-it-yourself "blind" wine-tasting? Hide the bottles in paper bags, number the bags, and keep score of the wines best liked. Then unveil the bottles to identify your choices. The wines you like least can be given to someone else to whom their flavor is more appealing.

If you don't tire in the process, you will be rewarded. For, as the late banker Carl Wente used to say to his

Wines for a "blind" tasting.

winegrower brothers, "Wine is like American business. When it's good, it's very good; when it's bad, it's still pretty good."

You may wonder, why not just ask a dealer to recommend a wine you will enjoy? This is a splendid idea and a convenient short cut, if, repeat if, you can find a dealer who enjoys wine himself and who regularly tastes the wines he sells. Avoid any dealer who doesn't care for wine, and the kind who only recommends the brands that give him the widest profit margin. (And never buy from a store that displays table wine in the window exposed to the sun.) Dealers who know and can discuss their wines are still lamentably scarce in most of the United States.

Let's focus on a first-time shopping expedition, and

assume that you contemplate buying a wine to serve with before-dinner hors d'oeuvres. This is an easy beginning because most people, even some store clerks, remember from TV movies or novels that one kind of wine often served before a meal is sherry. But the average store shelf contains many bottles of sherries variously labeled "amontillado," "cocktail," "cream," "dry," "fino," "oloroso," and some with just the word "sherry." Which to buy?

A good idea is to purchase two or three different sherry types whose labels state whether they are dry, medium-dry, or cream (which means sweet). Take them home and give your guests a choice. Note carefully which one was best liked. You will already be something of a sherry connoisseur!

"Hold on!" you may object. "Do I have to spend all that money?" The answer is: relax and buy freely, because in the average store three bottles of different sherries can be had for less than the price of a bottle of Scotch.

Giving your guests a choice of flavors is also advisable when you shop for a table wine to accompany a meal. Serving more than one kind is always a good idea, because just as you may like your steak served rare while your fellow diner prefers his well-done, individual tastes vary sharply among wines. Two different wines, if you buy them in half-bottles, cost little more than one bottle of a single type. If you are serving enough guests to use two bottles, two types will cost no more than one.

Which table wines to buy for a start? Try one bottle

each of chablis, or rosé, or red burgundy. If you prefer fancier names, select any flavor relatives of these types from those listed in the "Key to 362 Wines."

HOW TO AVOID SPOILED WINE

In selecting table wines, however, be as wise a shopper as you are in choosing other foods. Just as you are careful not to buy oversoft tomatoes or a tired head of lettuce, take similar precautions with this class of wine. This is because table wines are perishable—almost as perishable, under some conditions, as milk. Especially avoid buying a bottle whose label has grown yellow and frayed from overlong storage in the store.

Here I recommend the philosophy of the wise homemaker who went to her butcher and said: "I am having relatives in for dinner. How many chickens have you?"

The butcher counted: "Twelve."

"Pick out your eight toughest ones," she directed.

He did so with alacrity.

"I'll take the other four," she said.

The surest way to avoid getting a spoiled table wine is to buy it from a store that enjoys rapid turnover of its stock. In other words, get it from a merchant who sells a great deal of the specific type and brand you are buying. At this point I am avoiding questions about wines advertised on sale at sharp price reductions, and about how some wines improve with long aging in bottles. Those are covered in other chapters. Right now I am only warning against buying wines that are spoiled.

If the bottle you contemplate selecting has a cork

closure, note whether the store has kept it standing upright for a long time. In that position the cork soon dries out and admits air to begin spoiling the wine. Corked bottles should be stored lying horizontally to keep the cork moist and airtight. (Bottles with screw caps are better kept standing up.)

(And if you find that a wine you have bought is obviously spoiled, you should take it back to the dealer, who will return it to the vintner who sold it to him.)

It is easy to tell which wines are perishable and which are not. Just look at the labels, which tell the alcoholic content. You will see that the sherries and ports contain 17 or 18 to 20 percent alcohol, which preserves them effectively. Those are the types you can keep safely in that decanter on your sideboard. But the table-wine types, at only 9 to 14 percent, are more delicate, suffer most when exposed to heat or to direct sunlight. They also begin to lose quality soon after you open the bottles.

In your Bacchic shopping expeditions don't be a wine snob. You may be amazed to discover how delicious some of the lower-priced wines can be. There is no direct, inevitable relationship between a wine's price and its drinking quality. Unlike the situation among automobiles and most other kinds of merchandise, the flivvers among wines often taste better than the Cadillacs. This is especially likely to be the case when the highest-priced table wine in the store has stood too long on the shelf waiting for a buyer; it may be ruined and worthless. It sometimes happens that the most delectable wine in the entire stock is lurking on the bottom shelf, behind an unpretentious label, and bears one of the lowest price marks in the whole establishment. Take pride in the taste bargains you discover!

WHO SEALED THE BOTTLE?

This is a good point at which to digress briefly—assuming you have decided on the type of wine you want—to discuss choosing among brands. When different brands are offered, selling with equal frequency in the store, which should you buy?

Students of wine lore will probably choose the brand whose label says the wine was bottled at the winery where it was produced. On a French label, they look for the words *mise en bouteille au château*, a sign of authenticity which usually commands an extra price. On American wines such legends as "estate bottled," "produced and bottled by," and "bottled at the winery" have similar meanings. ("Made," as a later chapter explains, may or may not mean the same as "produced.") The German term for own-bottling is *Erzeuger Abfüllung*. However, wines so labeled are not necessarily the best buys, because some of the best wines some vintners sell are made for them by other wineries. I am inclined to rely more on the name and quality reputation of the vintner, importer, or European shipper than on whether he himself produced and bottled the wine.

Once you have found that one wine whose taste especially thrills you, the thing to do is run, don't walk, to the store where you got it, and buy more bottles from the same case. This is good advice because if you wait a few weeks to buy another bottle, it may not taste the same. Remember that few vintners are able to supply unchanging flavor in their wines from month to month, much less from year to year.

HOW MUCH TO BUY

How much to buy depends on when you are going to use it. If it is an expensive wine for a special occasion, buy the size of bottle you will use up the day you open and serve it in perfect condition. If you are going to store table wine or champagne at home for months, you need a cool place away from the furnace and from sunlight, where the corked bottles will lie on their sides. If you have such a space, you can save money, because wine is usually cheaper bought by the twelve-bottle case. Most stores will give you 10 percent off the bottle price. Ask them if it isn't so, because they seldom advertise the fact.

American wines come mainly in "fifth" (4/5 quart) or full quart bottles, but European table wines use somewhat smaller bottles, usually only 3/4 quart or an ounce less than that. So note the net contents before you buy, to make certain you are getting the quantity you want. (These size differences may be eliminated a few years hence. Our government plans by 1979 to change wine bottle sizes to the metric system of liters and centiliters, when a 75-centiliter bottle will replace the "fifth," a 3/8 liter will replace the "tenth," and a liter will replace the quart.)

The best store bargains in wine are the magnums ("double fifth") and the half-gallon and gallon jugs. The saving in bottling cost is passed on to you. Bought by the gallon, six ounces of table wine with your evening meal should cost you less than a pack of cigarettes or even some bottles of soda pop. Partly filled bottles or jugs left over from dinner will keep reasonably well in the refrigerator for several days. Leftover champagne, if tightly recorked and refrigerated, will retain some of its sparkle, too. If you keep your table wine in one of those new wide-mouthed carafes, you should cover the opening overnight with a piece of transparent plastic wrap.

Here is an additional economy tip: to get the by-the-gallon price and yet take your time about using the wine, transfer the contents of the jug into screw-capped bottles or half-bottles, carefully washing and drying them first. The refrigerator is also the best place for these.

I am often asked what quantity a dinner or party host should buy. A bottle of table wine ordinarily serves two, three, or four people at a meal. At my home, when the children are away, a bottle usually lasts two or three evenings for my wife and myself.

For larger groups, I have developed a formula from long experience. For weddings, I allow a bottle of champagne for each six persons, which supplies them slightly more than four ounces each, unless the guests include many teetotalers, in which circumstance a bottle can serve ten.

At a mixed-company banquet of many courses, with

several different wines on the menu, I allow an overall average of one bottle for three to four persons, but I expect to need a larger quantity of the first table wine served than of those that follow. If it is a dinner for a serious group of connoisseurs, I calculate pre-dinner champagne consumption at a fourth of a bottle per person, assorted table wines at a fourth-bottle each, and dessert wine at a bottle for eight persons. I have attended four-hour gourmet dinners, however, at which total wine consumption averaged almost two bottles per guest and from which everyone walked to his taxi-cab with a perfectly steady gait! The latter was because the wine was consumed slowly and with rich food.

But returning to the subject of ordinary purchases, there are seven prime secrets of successful wine shopping: Experiment freely, because it is fun, inexpensive, and instructive. Give your guests a choice among wines. Buy the bottle sizes that best fit your requirements and budget. Try the inexpensive as well as the more costly wines. Buy only at stores that have stored their wines properly; be sure they are in good condition. When you find a wine you especially like, buy more of the same immediately, but only in the quantity you can properly store. And finally, once again this reminder: if you are going to trust a dealer to select your purchases for you, be sure to pick one who regularly drinks wine himself.

5 / What's the Best Wine?

When you corner a wine expert and demand an answer to that oftenest asked of all wine questions, "What's the best wine?" you usually get this reply: "The best wine is the wine you like best; you are the only expert on your individual taste."

Don't blame him for being evasive. His answer makes sense, up to a point.

But what you really want, it seems to me—and I therefore presume to rephrase your question—is to know which country or which viticultural region produces the wines that impartial connoisseur experts (if anyone can be really impartial about taste) would regard as the finest of their kinds in the world. This chapter will attempt to answer that knotty question.

Past generations of connoisseurs in this country have accepted as gospel the opinions of British experts, that fine wines come only from Europe and that only France and Germany produce the truly great wines. Since the Second World War, however, this has begun to change.

Some of the famous wines of Europe have changed in character, not necessarily for the better. Meanwhile, extensive plantings of new vineyards and enormous advances in grape and wine technology have brought to notice wines from other parts of the world, including those of the United States.

SNEERS CHANGE TO PRAISE

California wines in particular, once scorned by dilettante writers who compared them to French *vin ordinaire,* have begun to outscore the costliest French and German vintages in "blind" comparative tastings, thousands of which have been held in this country in recent years. These developments have caused the dilettantes abruptly to change their sneers to effulgent praise. Now they are writing books and articles praising all American wines, even including the mass-produced, inexpensive kinds that are sold in jugs.

This kind of reverse snobbery, this abrupt change from scorn to praise, has started serious students of wine wondering about what talents qualify those who pass as wine experts and what flavor characteristics really constitute quality in wines. These added questions will be discussed here and in the chapter that follows, but let us accept for the moment that there must be many qualified experts among the oenophiles who serve on the juries of the wine-quality competitions held periodically in various parts of the world.

There has never been an international judging in

which all of the world's principal wines were impartially compared, with their labels hidden, solely on their individual merits. Since such a competition is not likely to be held, I am going to venture how I believe it would result. My imaginary jury for this imaginary quality sweepstakes will consist of the several hundred Europe-minded connoisseurs, professionals and experienced amateurs, with whom I have tasted wines during the past forty years. I think most of them, if they were to read this, would agree with most of my hypothetical awards.

WHO THE CHAMPIONS ARE

France would surely receive the grand prix for champagnes, sauternes, and Côte d'Or red burgundies and would win several medals for the best clarets of Bordeaux.

Germany would win the Oscar for the most delicate, most fragrant White ("Johannisberg") Rieslings, dry to medium-sweet.

Spain and Portugal would walk away with the dry sherry and aged port awards, and Madeira with the prize for the wines that bear that island's name.

Italy could not be denied the medal for its sparkling Muscat, nor the prizes for chianti, barolo, and marsala.

California would triumph with the world's finest Cabernet Sauvignons, dry Gewürztraminers, Chenin Blancs, Barberas, and dry rosés. It would tie with France for fine white burgundies made of the Char-

donnay grape, for the best Gamay Noirs (the grape
of Beaujolais), and for its nonsparkling wines of the
various Muscat-flavored grapes.

Each region obviously would excel with its exclusive
specialties: Hungary with its tokays; California with
its angelica, Zinfandel, Pinot St. George, Charbono,
Emerald Riesling, and Ruby Cabernet; New York,
Ohio, and Ontario with their best champagnes and
white table wines, which have the unique aroma of
their native American grapes, but only a hint of them
in their aftertaste. Late entries from the young vineyards of true Old World wine grapes in Washington,
Oregon, New York, and Ohio might be runners-up
for some White Riesling medals. Australia, Chile,
South Africa, Yugoslavia, and Greece each would
probably capture one or more prizes, especially Australia, which has improved its wines tremendously since
the Second World War. Russia's extensive viticultural
industry, whose best products have not yet appeared
in the West, conceivably could score, as well.

In a hypothetical runoff for the world championship
in single bottles regardless of type, the votes would
most likely be evenly divided between some one vintage of great age and bouquet from one of the hundreds
of celebrated vineyards of Burgundy's Côte de Nuits
and another from some historic château in the Pauillac
commune of Bordeaux. Having tasted many long-lived
great wines from these two best red wine districts of
France, I imagine I might vote for these noble entries,
too.

WHAT CONSTITUTES QUALITY?

What constitutes quality in a wine? Every expert has his own set of criteria, but condensed from many lengthy explanations, they amount to this:

First, a wine must be free of defects, of which experts can detect many kinds, including some that do not actually detract from a wine's enjoyable taste. Of course, there must be no off-odors or tastes, but, wines being perishable, anyone may occasionally encounter a bottle that has lost quality or is actually spoiled.

The wine's color must be appealing, and it must be brilliant, because the eye conditions our other senses of taste.

A wine should have fragrance as well as flavor to be fine. This is because most of our sense of taste is not in our mouth, but in our nose. It must have either the fruity fragrance called "aroma" or the winy odor called "bouquet." Both together are called the wine's "nose."

Next, the nose and taste should be interesting, should invite more than a first taste. A wine with only a single flavor may please many people who are not experts, but will lack interest to the connoisseur. To be truly fine, a wine must have complexity, flavors within flavors, the experts say. It should produce different, partially hidden taste sensations with each smell or sip.

A wine's taste must also be in balance, with all of its qualities married into a harmonious whole. If it

49

is sweet, the sweetness must be balanced by acidity (tartness); otherwise it will taste flat. If dry, it must not be rough or harsh. A wine also must have "body" (substance, mouth-filling quality, texture) from its content of grape solids. Wines lacking in body taste thin.

Young wines should have freshness, be thrillingly delicious, richly aromatic with the perfume of grapes. Old wines should have intriguing nuances from the flavor compounds that form gradually as a wine ages in cask and bottle. Flavors and odors come also from the wood of which a cask is made, especially from different species of oak. Woody tastes may be too prominent in young wines, but added years in the bottle may soften and marry them with winy tastes.

Still more elements add to flavor: the zestful personality of a dominant variety of grape; the glycerine-like smoothness that some whites possess; the just-right degree of bitterness and astringency a pink or a red wine seems to need.

Finally and above all, a fine wine must give the connoisseur pleasure, which all of its characteristics combine to produce.

Yet there are millions of Americans whose tastes do not agree with those of the experts and connoisseurs. The Latin author of the saying *"De gustibus non disputandum"* ("there is no accounting for tastes") was almost surely referring to wine. Individual preferences differ to extremes in wines as they do in foods. Philadelphians like scrapple; Hawaiians like poi, and Scots enjoy haggis, the recipe for which would make you gag. You may like your steak blood-rare but I prefer mine cooked through. I recall reading that Frederick the Great liked champagne in his coffee with a bit of mustard stirred in, and that Columbus often put salt in his wine. The resin-flavored wine called retsina is popular in Greece, and some is regularly produced in California for the Greek-American trade. I know some home winemakers who reject any wine that does not taste of bitter grape stems.

No self-anointed authority can tell you what to like. One of the strangest aspects of viniana in America is that so many depend on the opinion of so few as to what is good.

On the other hand, there is also such a thing as the training of taste. Our flavor preferences change with experience and with age. We find ourselves liking things we once disliked at first taste. When I began drinking coffee I loaded it with sugar and cream, but I gradually reduced the sugar to zero and now I drink it black. Youths are the principal buyers of the bubbly sweet pop wines, which my connoisseur friends despise. There is now statistical evidence that many youths switch within months from pop wines to the traditional dry mealtime types.

We learn to appreciate wines much as we learn the appreciation of art, music, and literature. Your first time at the opera may have seemed a jumble of sound and story, but with study and exposure to classical music you may have become an opera lover. The more we come to know, the more we enjoy.

51

OTHER THINGS THAT COUNT

Let us make some closer comparisons among "the best wines."

Climate is what most affects quality in wines. Soil is also important, but good soils for grapes can be found almost anywhere, while ideal climates cannot.

French champagnes and burgundies and the white wines of Germany are high in acidity, aroma, and delicate flavors because they grow in the northernmost, coolest vineyards of western Europe. Champagne and Burgundy are so cool, in fact, that the Pinot Noir and Chardonnay grown there often fail to reach full ripeness, and in most years need to have sugar added in order to make sound wines. Yet there are no rivals anywhere for the best French champagnes nor for the best red wines grown on the sunny Burgundian hillside named the Côte d'Or (golden slope). The same applies for the same reason to the German rhine and moselle wines made of the White Riesling grape.

The sweet golden wines of the Bordeaux locality called Sauternes are unique because of a certain mold, the *Botrytis cinerea* or *pourriture noble,* which grows naturally in that humid though sunny climate on the surface of overripe Sémillon and Sauvignon Blanc grapes. It sweetens and imparts to them an extra-pleasing flavor unrelated to that of the grapes. The same mold grows on the White Riesling in Germany, where it is called the Edelfäule, and also sometimes produces fine medium-sweet Riesling wines in California and

New York. Yet none of them has ever resembled the sweet sauternes of Bordeaux.

(This always reminds me of the New York wine salesman who once read a book, and enthralled by his newly acquired knowledge, announced to all and sundry that the best wines are made from moldy grapes!)

Vineyards in California's coastal districts enjoy long, rainless summers. They receive more hours of sunshine per season than the top French and German districts, yet they are also cooled by Pacific Ocean winds and fogs. This climate is the envy of Europe because it brings to balanced ripeness Cabernet Sauvignon, Chardonnay, and the other wine grapes in which the Golden State excels. No sugar need ever be added to California grapes. But when the same noble grapes are planted in California's hot Central Valley, they produce only ordinary wines. In the warmer climate, grape varieties of high acidity, such as French Colombard, Barbera, and Ruby Cabernet, produce better wines than the cool-weather grapes can.

There are other factors besides climate. Spanish fino, amontillado, and oloroso sherries and manzanillas excel for two different reasons. Their "nutty," "oxidized," or "madeirized" taste comes first from a yeast called *flor*, which grows naturally (perhaps because of climate) on the surface of wines in partially filled casks in the vicinity of Jerez de la Frontera, for which sherry is named. It comes second from the extra years of aging these Spanish wines are given in *soleras* of old Ameri-

53

can oak casks, in which very old sherries are blended gradually with younger ones. The similar wines of Madeira and Marsala and most American sherries are also "oxidized" and "nutty," but from aging at warm temperatures. The *flor* flavor is something else again. Only in recent years have *flor* sherries been developed in the United States.

But why all the emphasis on California, whose wine-growing history dates back only to 1769? Why not consider the eastern states, where Lord Delaware launched the industry in 1619, and the Midwest, where Ohio's vineyards and wines were praised in Longfellow's *Ode to Catawba Wine?* The answer is that California, besides producing three fourths of the wine consumed in the nation, is the one state that grows only the true wine grapes, the *Vitis vinifera,* from which all the best wines of Europe are made. In the rest of the United States, the principal grapes grown are of the *Vitis labrusca,* varieties of American wild grapes with their pronounced grapy or "foxy" taste. Labrusca wines have not been duplicated anywhere else in the world, but are used mostly to make sweet and semi-sweet wines. Lately a different group of grapes, the French-American hybrids, crosses between Vinifera and American wild grapes, have been planted in many of the eastern and midwestern states. They are making dry, European-type wines that have no Labrusca taste.

A double kinship exists between American and European wines. Cuttings of the Old World's grapevines were transplanted to California; and most vines in Europe are grafted on roots of wild American vines, transplanted from this country to combat a vine pest which destroyed most of Europe's vineyards in the last half of the nineteenth century. The pest is a vine louse called phylloxera, to which American wild vines are immune.

America has two advantages over Europe—climates more hospitable to grapes, and the will to apply science to winemaking, while most Europeans are content to continue making wine in cobwebbed cellars by the primitive methods of their ancestors.

Undeniably, Europe offers a greater number and variety of individual superlative wines than America can. Out of the billions of gallons produced in the scores of different regions on the older continent you would expect this to be the case. This makes it all the more remarkable that American wines have begun to catch up.

HOW DOES A $5000 WINE TASTE?

Now we come to the delicate subject of price.

There is the story of the man in Chicago who inherited a generations-old bottle of wine that was reputed to be worth $5000.

"When are you going to open it?" someone asked.

"I don't know," he replied, "there hasn't been a coronation in our house yet."

You may wonder what such a $5000 bottle would taste like if it were opened. More likely than not, it would taste like vinegar, or worse.

Rare, famous fine wines sell for astronomical prices partly because they are fine but partly also because

55

they are rare. When a famous vineyard produces a mere few hundred cases to supply the world, buyers bid up the price; it is supply and demand at work.

San Francisco *Chronicle* columnist Herb Caen explains it: "Wine is one of the few remaining luxury items worth paying too much for. We enjoy it most when we pay more than it is worth." He is right that our taste for a wine is influenced by its price.

A wine merchant friend of mine expresses it differently. "I sometimes wonder how much the most expensive bottles in my stock would be worth," he says, "if their labels happened to fall off and get lost."

Some buyers pay two-digit prices for famous wines they have not yet learned to appreciate. I sometimes wish I could give them a simple test. They would taste three wines from numbered glasses, one containing a twenty-dollar wine, another a two-dollar, and the third a one-dollar wine. I keep wondering which of the three they would choose as "the best."

Wine-buying is still self-conscious in Britain and the United States. Anxious to be regarded as buyers of only the best, and suspicious of any alcoholic beverages that are low in price, many people I know are buying expensive labels rather than wines. "A moderate-priced wine that looks expensive" is what some of them seek. What they get in response is often grossly overpriced.

On the other hand, I know many professional vintners who make and sell five-dollar-a-bottle wines, but who buy everyday jug wines to drink with their meals at home.

A fact not yet generally known in the United States

is that young, fresh, everyday table wine costs less than milk to produce. Wine comes from grapes, which grow on vines. One does not need a cow to produce wine. Everyday table wine would sell in stores for less than milk in this country, as it does in Spain, if it were not for the exorbitant per-gallon taxes, dealer-license fees, and political restrictions that make wine distribution inefficient.

Old and fine wines, on the other hand, are works of art—nature's art and the vintner's art. They belong in the field of art. They cost more to produce than young wines do. Fine wines are intended to be served and appreciated on special occasions, as the works of art they are.

WINERIES LARGE AND SMALL

A small producer of fine table wine grows a noble grape variety in a cool but sunny climate. He may hope to get three tons per acre, compared to twelve tons from a hardier variety grown in a hot climate to make everyday wine. He hand-prunes and repeatedly thins his vines to get fewer but finer grapes of perfect sugar-and-acid balance. When his grapes begin to ripen, he tests them daily. When the moment of ideal ripeness arrives, he picks them by hand, but only those that are perfect; he leaves the rest on the vine. He carries them in small boxes to the winery, crushes and ferments them immediately. He uses the free-run juice with the barest minimum of press wine. He babies his wine, aging it first in small casks, then in the costliest oak barrels. When it is ripe for bottling, he uses the longest, costliest corks. Then he ages the wine again for years in the bottles. For every additional year of age he gives his vintage, he has to double the capacity of his winery. His wine is more expensive than others of its type.

Bigger wineries are more efficient. By using scientific quality controls, automated mass production, and mass marketing, they are able to deliver at moderate prices wines you might not distinguish, if you removed the labels, from the small grower's more expensive wine. The small winery may keep separate each cask of its wine under a special label. The larger winery may blend its best casks with the rest to give you uniformly good wine even if not so high in peaks of quality. Then there is the romance of the little vineyard which, associated with its hand-made wine and higher price, adds remarkably to its delicious taste.

A large vintner, discussing this with me at dinner in his home one evening, said: "No doubt about it, the buggy was more romantic than the Chrysler Imperial. But does anyone want to trade his Chrysler for a buggy?" While he spoke, I noted that the wine on his table came from one of the romantic little wineries of California.

"GOOD," "FINE," OR "GREAT"?

To most European winegrowers and consumers, the best wine is the one that is highest in alcoholic content. The French Government's regulations governing appellation-controlled wines grant the highest labeling designations to the most alcoholic wines. Yet the finest wines of France are not grown in the warmest French climates, where the grapes grow extra sweet, but in the cooler climates, where the sugar and alcoholic contents are low.

To the great California viticulturist Dr. Albert J. Winkler, the best wine is the one with longevity, the one that has the capacity to improve with age, to develop the combination of mellow smoothness, the complex of flavors within flavors, and the great bouquet of a fine old wine.

Not all wines can be "best," but all wines that are sound and palatable are *good*. A wine markedly superior in taste, nose, and balance to good wines is *fine*. A fine wine which gives the connoisseur such pure delight to his senses as to be unforgettable, deserves to be called *great*.

You are the connoisseur; the wine you consider great is your best wine.

6 / How to Taste Wine

The late Almond R. Morrow, who first taught me how to taste, used to tell the famous story of the three monks who were winemakers at a monastery in Germany.

One of the monks, tasting from a cask of wine, thought it tasted somehow of wood, but not of the oak from which the cask was made. He tasted it again and again and became more and more sure that there was an off-taste of some kind. He called the second monk, who tasted and re-tasted the wine, and said yes, there was an off-taste, but it was of something metallic, not of wood. They couldn't agree, so they called in the third monk. He said, after much more tasting, that the off-taste seemed to him like leather. The three of them kept on tasting until the cask was empty, so they finally opened it to see what might be wrong. There in the bottom of the cask was a key tied with a leather thong to a piece of wood.

Although the German story is a bit hard to believe,

there is substance to at least some of the stories that are still told about Al Morrow himself. He is said to have named on many occasions, by tasting a wine, the hillside on which grew the grapes from which the wine was made. Morrow was the taster for the California Wine Association before Prohibition and bought wines each year from hundreds of different vineyards throughout that state. Once, on detecting that a wine had an unusually flat taste—apparently the result of overcropped vines—Morrow decided the farmer must have mortgaged his vineyard. He ventured an estimate of the amount of the mortgage, which—legend says—proved to be correct.

I have known many professional and amateur experts to perform less remarkable tasting feats than Morrow's, and on occasion have myself identified the source and name of a wine with no other clue than its smell and taste. But I should confess that this was really easy to do, because each time the wine had some peculiarity, usually a defect, which I happened to remember. You may be certain that anyone who identifies a wine completely "blind" has tasted it or a similar wine a short time before.

Anyone can become an expert taster if he has normal senses of sight, smell, and taste; if he samples enough wines and pays close attention while doing so; if he remembers what he has tasted—and if he also knows a few simple but essential professional tasting techniques.

It is worthwhile to learn these techniques—although

they require more concentration than the average wine lover may care to apply—because our tasting experiences tell us some interesting things about ourselves.

For example, few people realize that each of us sees, smells, and tastes the same colors, odors, and flavors differently from anyone else. This, incidentally, is what makes it easy for fake experts to get by, since nobody can contradict what you say you do or do not taste.

We also perceive colors, smells, and tastes somewhat differently from day to day, at different times of day, in rooms of different temperatures, in different kinds of light, and even in different kinds of company. You will find these things true of yourself if you take up wine tasting and do it right.

When you drink a wine, all of your taste sensations combine into a single impression of whether you like or dislike it, and to what degree. Using the professional tasting techniques tells you why. The professional separates the total impression of a wine into the single qualities and defects that were described in the preceding chapter, which taken individually help him determine "what's the best wine."

You first taste a wine with your eyes. Hold it to the light. Is it clear, or brilliant, or hazy, or dull? Has it viscosity? Does it adhere to the sides of the glass, forming what the French call the "legs" of the wine? Examine its color. Is it correct for this wine type, or is it lacking in some respect? Make notes, because each thing your eyes perceive will be part of your total evaluation of the wine.

If perchance you question whether sight affects taste, try the following experiment: Pour the same wine into two glasses. Add to one glass a few drops of tasteless vegetable color. Then ask someone else to tell you which wine he prefers. To him, each will have a different taste. (Yes, I am among the many who have been victims of this test.)

Second, examine the wine with your nose. Swirl it in your glass to vaporize its volatile odors, because they must reach your olfactory nerve cells, which are buried in the mucous lining high in the nasal passages above your nose. Are there any odd or off-odors (yeasty, stemmy, vinegary, musty, raisiny, rubbery, oxidized)? Has the wine an aroma of fruit? What kind? Has it bouquet—intense, moderate, little, or none? Again note down what you have found.

Third, after resting briefly, it is time to examine the wine in your mouth. Chew it, slurp air through your teeth and the wine, again to volatilize and send the thus-intensified odors through your rear nasal passages to your nerve cells of smell. Meanwhile, the onion-shaped taste buds at the tip of your tongue are telling you whether the wine is sweet and to what degree; those at the sides of the tongue perceive whether it is salty; others whether it is tart and how tart; while bitterness is perceived at the back of the tongue. Only these four flavors—sweet, salt, acid, and bitter—can be sensed by the taste buds. Still other nerve endings in your mouth perceive sensations of heat or cold, smoothness or roughness, astringency, and the wine's texture or "body." The rest of taste is in the nose. Our olfactory cells are said to be able to detect seventeen thousand different odors. I have read that half of the impressions of conscious life come from the sense of smell; it is our keenest sense. If you have a bad head cold, you cannot distinguish the flavor of a slice of onion from that of raw potato.

Next, empty your mouth; expert tasters do not swallow. Note what you have just learned, and now notice still another thing—the aftertaste, the flavor sensations after the wine has left your mouth. Aftertaste tells you things about a wine you may not have been able to detect before.

(Why doesn't a taster swallow? First, because if the wine remained in his system its volatile substances could reduce the keenness of his taste for a second wine. Second, because downing several glassfuls in a short time could put him out of action for the day. Yes, an occasional drop of wine will find its way down his throat, but I have tasted fifty wines in a morning without feeling the slightest alcoholic effect. My body had metabolized the minuscule amount I had ingested, sooner than it could have been felt.)

Now assemble your notes, the total of all your impressions. Professional and amateur tasters since Al Morrow's day have adopted a convenient method of recording their notes. They use a more or less standard 20-point or 50-point scorecard. They give or subtract points or fractions for each quality or defect of a wine. Here is a typical 20-point scorecard:

	Maximum points
Appearance (brilliant, clear, cloudy?)	2
Color (correct? browning?)	2
Aroma (odor of grape variety)	2
Bouquet (aged, oxidized?)	2
Acescence (not vinegary, sour)	2
Acidity (fruit acid in balance)	2
Sugar (sweet or dry for this wine type)	1
Body (full or light?)	1
Flavor (grape character, oak, sulphur?)	2
Astringency (tannin content high or low?)	2
General quality (balanced? overall impression)	2

A total of 17 to 20 points means a wine is considered outstanding; 13–16 indicates standard quality; 9–12 means defective but acceptable; less than 9 means unacceptable.

Tasting isn't easy. It is often done carelessly, which may explain the strange wine-judging results you sometimes read about. It requires meticulous preparation. Have the glasses been stored with proper ventilation? I have smelled musty odors in a series of wines, only to discover that the glasses had been standing upside down on a shelf in a stuffy closet for a week. Has each glass been thoroughly washed, and then rinsed with the wine to be tasted? (Smell the empty glass before you pour.) Are the wines at the same temperatures (moderately cool) so that they can be compared?

65

I often hear amateur tasters discussing a wine before they have written their notes, a blunder that can influence their results. At some wineries, each taster works isolated in an air-conditioned booth under a special diffused light. Numbered glasses are placed before him through a window that opens in the wall.

Seldom do any two tasters agree entirely in their appraisals of wine. This is why wineries' taste panels and teams of judges of wine quality competitions consist of at least three members. Teams of five are preferred.

The mistake most often made is to taste two wines in succession without giving the olfactory nerves a rest. Few amateur tasters realize how quickly their sense of smell gets tired. They can learn this by being reminded of the times they have entered a room with a strong odor inside, such as a kitchen in which cauliflower is cooking. After two minutes in the room, they may no longer perceive the smell. But if they leave the room, and remain outside for two minutes, and then return, the odor strikes them with full force again. The professional taster knows he must rest for two minutes between his tastings of two different wines. Meanwhile he rinses his mouth with unchilled water, sometimes also chewing a bit of bread to remove the last vestige of the preceding wine. (He does not eat cheese, which adds to the pleasure of drinking wine, but detracts from the acuity of taste.) Incidentally, our sense of smell is keenest when we are hungry, which is why professional tasting is usually done before lunch.

Individuals' responses to a wine differ mainly because each of us has different threshold levels of sensitivity to different flavors. Wines contain some three hundred natural compounds, and your thresholds of sensitivity to some substances are higher or lower than your neighbor's. For example, some people are super-sensitive to a normal amount of sulphur in wine, while others do not notice it at all. I, on the other hand, am moderately sensitive to sulphur and can only detect the normal amount by noticing a faint biting sensation in the upper part of my nose.

There have been wine judges who were partially taste-blind but who were unaware of the fact. Their difficulty was detected by the "triangle taste test," which measures one's ability to identify specific flavors and odors.

Anyone who does serious tasting should take this test. To half of a bottle of wine, add a minute amount

The Triangular Taste Test   Number the glasses with a lipstick or grease pencil. Two of the glasses contain the same wine, the third glass an almost identical wine. Taster must identify the odd one. The test is repeated *seven* times. Five correct is "passing."

of some substance naturally present in wine, such as tartaric or citric acid. The person to be tested for his ability to perceive acidity levels is presented with three numbered glasses. Two contain the original wine, the third the identical wine with the added acid. He must identify the odd glass. Because he might do so by chance, the same test with the samples renumbered is administered to him seven times. Five correct out of seven is a passing mark. To qualify as a wine judge, he should pass the same test for perception of different levels of sugar, tannin, acetic acid (vinegar), sulfur dioxide, and alcohol.

A more popular test is to be blindfolded and try to distinguish a red wine from a white by taste. (Concentrate on detecting the different levels of tannin content if you want to pass.)

It is easy to be fooled. Repeated testimony by professional experts was that the wine scandals of the 1970s at Bordeaux and in Italy occurred because the professional tasters were unable to tell the adulterated wines from genuine wines by taste. A trained tasting panel at the University of California was found to be wrong at least a third of the time in trying to identify by blind-tasting the grape varieties from which experimental wines had been made. To anyone, a wine may taste sweet when a test of its sugar content would show it is dry, the reason being that glycerols in the wine may have sensitized the taste buds that perceive sweet tastes. Sometimes a wine will have an unpleasant odor, but may recover and become delicious if allowed to rest for several days. The wine may be suffering from bottle-sickness, which can occur when it is first bottled, or after it has traveled for several days.

Does smoking interfere with tasting ability? Yes, a smoke screen will interfere if you puff while you taste, but there are many regular smokers among my expert-taster friends. I always extinguish my pipe at least an hour before I do any tasting.

Which sex has the keener taste is a question the feminist movement has raised. Several men in the wine industry have admitted to me privately that their wives excel them as tasters, but only Philip Wagner of the Boordy Vineyard in Maryland has confessed this in print. Apparently nobody has yet been brave enough to try to settle this question by any measured research. Meanwhile the number of women graduates from schools of enology has grown steadily in recent years, and several leading wineries now employ female tasters.

Taste blindness has been shown by recent studies to be a much more common ailment than has generally been supposed. It usually is caused by illnesses in which the olfactory nerves are left impaired. Reduced taste acuity can also be caused by depression and by dietary unbalance, such as by a deficiency of zinc. Cases of the latter have lately been cured by prescribing diets rich in zinc, especially a diet of fish.

I am deferring to a later chapter the answers to two additional questions that are constantly asked about wine tasting: how to tell how long the contents of a given bottle are likely to improve with age, and second, how to tell just when an aging wine is likely to reach its peak of quality and be ready to be opened and enjoyed. These two intriguing subjects are primarily of interest to those who acquire wines for future drinking, and they therefore are discussed in the chapter about wine cellars.

Some of the confusion about wine tasting can be blamed on the poetic language connoisseur writers employ in describing the flavor qualities they find in the wines they taste. How can their readers find accurate flavor meanings in such terms as big, beguiling, broad-shouldered, charming, distinguished, elegant, enticing, finesse, flexible, graceful, masculine, rich, supple, and suave? "Tell me, please," my wife once asked me while scanning a wine magazine, "how exactly does 'finesse' taste in a wine?" In an attempt to simplify wine-flavor descriptions, I have included in the Glossary at the end of this book the several taste-descriptive terms on the precise meanings of which most professionals appear to agree.

Is serious, accurate wine tasting worth the effort for you? If not, perhaps my detailed listing of the techniques and problems has at least earned your appreciation for what our professional tasters endure.

7 / Kinds for Every Use

Among all the beverages of mankind no other offers so bounteous a variety of flavors and uses as does wine. To quote the otherwise matter-of-fact language of *The Wine Study Course:*

"Wine is the one beverage that is fittingly used to celebrate the holy Mass, to accompany the workman's meal, to observe a memorable occasion, to inspire the poet, to minister to the sick, to welcome guests who drop in, to enhance the flavor of cooking, to mix drinks that cool the hot summer day or warm the cold winter evening, to make the connoisseur's banquet perfect, to launch ships, to toast beggar or king. No other beverage has had such universal recommendations through the ages."

This somewhat flowery tribute once brought me a telephone call from an impatient *Wine Study Course* student. "I'm not launching a ship or celebrating anything," the lady complained. "My husband's old-fogy boss, who likes your stuff, is coming to dinner tonight.

Just tell me in one word or less the kind of wine I've got to buy." I prescribed a bottle each of chablis and burgundy, and silently thanked the lady for teaching me thereafter to keep my wine recommendations less ambiguous, and to suggest, instead, specific wines for specific uses.

This chapter is addressed especially to the new wine consumer. If you have not yet discovered the many different ways in which wines can add richly to your pleasure, the suggestions that follow should be of some help.

To begin, I advise you to buy an all-purpose wine and let the rest come naturally. Such an all-purpose beverage is the pink table wine called rosé (pronounced ro-ZAY). Frank Schoonmaker, the importer and wine author who first popularized this type in the United States, deserves the undying gratitude of Americans for doing so. Rosé is the one wine you can bring out of your refrigerator and serve at any time for any use without a brow-wrinkling thought as to whether you have made an acceptable choice. Simply chill it, open, and pour.

But you probably would like some additional prescriptions, so let us start with your before-dinner hour.

The simplest answer is sherry. At our home I keep two kinds handy—dry, which I prefer—and cream for guests who like sweet. Most of them enjoy it chilled or at least cool, or even over ice.

But variety adds spice, so bring out whatever else you happen to have—port, Dubonnet, dry or sweet vermouth, and white wine if you have some already chilled. Some people may question my inclusion of port because of the widespread impression that before-meal drinks must be "dry." If you have traveled in Europe, however, you probably have noticed that the favorite apéritifs on the continent are mostly sweet. (France alone imports more port from Portugal than the Portuguese drink.)

How about something extra glamorous when you have cocktail-time guests? Serve them champagne, which isn't as expensive as you think. There is no bother, nothing to mix; just open the chilled bottle and pour. For people who know wines, choose the kind labeled "brut"; for others use the "extra dry," which is slightly sweet.

In summer you can delight your guests with the lovely light drink called a Kir, which has become popular since the Second World War. It is named for the late war-hero priest, Canon Félix Kir of Dijon. All you need is well-chilled chablis and the black-currant liqueur called crème de cassis. Add to each glass of chablis just enough cassis to turn the wine's color to a blushing pink, or a bit more if you wish it sweet. Buy the small bottle of cassis; in the large size the taste may not stay fresh.

There also are wine cocktails that you can mix and keep in the refrigerator ready to serve. Best known is the bamboo cocktail, which is two parts dry sherry, one part each of dry and sweet vermouth, with a dash of Angostura bitters. My own favorite is the A. R.

Morrow cocktail: Mix equal parts of sherry, dry vermouth, sweet vermouth, chablis, and brandy, and store in the refrigerator for a few days. None of my guests, including the most hardened cocktail drinkers, has ever failed to praise this drink.

Enough about before-meal drinking; now how about ornamenting the everyday family meal? If you won't settle for all-purpose rosé alone, put bottles of dry red and white wines on the table, and let folks help themselves. Specific kinds? Any kinds described as dry or medium-dry in the Key to 362 Wines. Your family's specific preferences will soon emerge, and thereafter you can buy their favorites in the large economy sizes, the magnum and the jugs.

Let's go on to the holiday or guest dinner, at which you want to serve a very special wine. For such events I bring out the famous, expensive bottles I keep in my cellar. This is what these works of the vintner's art are for.

And since wines are my special interest, I like to match the wine with the main dish. What the Wine and Food Society does is appoint a committee, which first holds a pilot dinner. The committee members have the entire test meal served while they taste different wines with each course and make their selections for the future Lucullan repast. You needn't go to such fussy extremes. If your main dish is red meat, serve any dry red. If it is fish or fowl, serve any dry or medium-dry white. Add rosé while you are at it, and you have insured your guests' delight.

Want your dinner to be supremely festive? Then,

instead of only still wines, include champagne, either white, pink, or red.

An extra fillip, to backtrack a course or two, is to serve a special wine with the soup. The obvious choice is sherry, whose flavor blends so famously with this course that you will find sherry already an ingredient in most really fine canned soups.

When it comes to dessert, the choice of a wine is also easy because desserts are normally sweet. Ports, cream sherries, and the muscat types are also sweet. My own favorite dessert-time wines are the sweet sauternes.

Members of my family like assorted cheeses toward the end of a festive meal. Most flavorful cheeses taste best with either a hearty dry red wine or a mellow red port.

Moving on to the bridge table, sherry is the traditional wine to sip between bids. In my neighborhood, however, wines served at bridge parties include the light sweet muscat types, angelica, and white port.

In hot, stuffy weather, drinks for your guests should be long, well-diluted, and cool. They can range from the simple *spritzer* (wine and soda) to wine lemonade (lemonade with added red wine or rosé) and to the many wine punches, recipes for which you often find at beverage stores. Wine can also be mixed with any kind of soda pop, especially the lemon-flavored types.

But for a warm moonlit evening the classic cold wine drink is sangría, named by the Spanish for blood, *sangre.* You can buy it in bottles, but by far the best is the sangría you prepare yourself. In a pitcher with

75

plenty of ice put sliced fruits, berries, fruit juices, sugar to taste, also water or soda if you wish, and then add any dry red wine.

Wine for the barbecue is easily chosen; it is usually dry red or rosé. If you prefer white with those sizzling charcoal-broiled chickens, keep the bottles chilled in a tub of ice.

The versatility of wine extends to cold winter nights. A traditional warmer-up in ski country is hot mulled wine. It is dry red wine sweetened and spiced with cloves, lemon peel, powdered ginger, and allspice. Boil the spicy ingredients in water with sugar, stirring until the sugar is dissolved; simmer briefly; let stand for the spices to settle, and then strain. Now add orange juice, lemon juice, and lastly the red wine. Heat gently (don't boil) and serve in hot mugs.

How about quantity punches for parties? The best known, of course, is champagne punch. But here I protest; there can be no excuse for wasting good champagne in a mixture where this effervescent wine loses its identity and where bubbles can be gotten from sparkling water at much less expense. Use dry white wines to mix the punch; then add club soda, and finally a single bottle of champagne for the use of its glamorous name. Scores of punch recipes are usually available in stores, calling for such ingredients as fresh and frozen fruits, sherbets, concentrates, canned juices, and liqueurs.

But aren't there also specific wines which fit certain uses better than all others do? Indeed there are. For example, red port is the traditional wine to sip while puffing a fragrant cigar. Had it not been for the time-honored British custom of after-dinner port for the gentleman, while the ladies retired from the table, the Portuguese port industry would not be what it is today. Port also has a special affinity for walnuts. Once you taste this combination, you will never again reach for your nutcracker without first bringing out a bottle of port.

While history fails to record the specific wine type with which ladies of Elizabethan times bathed their faces to improve their complexions, we do know that Anna Held's legendary wine bath could only have been taken in champagne. And Lucien B. Johnson, the champion wine salesman of the pre-Prohibition years, always insisted that champagne is not the wine with which to woo a lady fair. "Champagne only makes folks talkative," Lucien used to say, "but burgundy, warmed to the temperature of the room, makes people affectionate. Yes, burgundy is the only *love* wine!"

You cannot marry off your daughter respectably these days without serving champagne at the reception. Here I usually suggest to the bride's parents that they buy the less expensive kind, because the caterers usually hide the labels with napkins, anyway. This also applies to ship launchings, where the champagne just goes to waste.

At Jewish holiday feasts the wine that flows must be *Kosher l'Pesach,* but fortunately the rabbis nowadays put their *hechsher* seals on a complete variety of wine types, so that the celebrants do have a choice.

For the sick, the oftenest-prescribed wine seems to

be port, which is also the base for some of the proprietary medicines sold in drugstores, including some of the old-time favorite tonics. Port again gets the call in the pleasant custom of laying down a bottle of wine when a child is born, to age until his twenty-first birthday.

And completing the round of the clock, port is also the favorite nightcap wine because of its reputed ability to induce a pleasant night's sleep.

But wait! How about morning wines? It would be a grave omission indeed to skip champagne breakfasts and Sunday brunches. For the former, serve a choice of white and pink champagnes. For the latter, although rhine wine types and champagne are both popular, I personally like the dash of color added by rosé.

And speaking of wine in the morning, there once was a famous connoisseur who always began the day by brushing his teeth with sauterne.

Perhaps you now expect to find, upon turning the next page, one of those charts often found in stores, dictating precisely which wine should accompany each course of a meal and each kind of food. It isn't there. I have been preaching for forty years that nobody needs these formidable charts. They have discouraged millions of householders from even beginning to serve wine.

In this chapter I have more than once recommended red wines with hearty foods and white wines with chicken or fish. When you think of this, however, you will see the reason is so simple that my advice really wasn't needed. The flavors of food themselves call for certain flavors in wines. Why does a hearty steak or roast taste best with a dry, puckery red wine? The obvious answer is that you want a wine with enough flavor so that you can taste it all the while you are eating your flavorful, sizzling steak. The much milder taste of a cool, delicate white wine would be overpowered by the meat flavor if you drank it with a chunk of hearty roast. Isn't it equally obvious that to enhance the delicate flavor of oysters, or of a delicate fish dish, the best selection would be a glass of equally delicate, tart White Riesling, or muscadet, graves, rheingau, French Colombard, or moselle? Shouldn't the wine for your Easter dinner be medium-sweet, rather than dry, in order to blend most deliciously with your sweet-garnished baked ham?

Yes, there are classic taste-harmonies, such as coffee with doughnuts, mustard with hot dogs, beer with sausage and sauerkraut, maple syrup with hotcakes, the slice of lemon on the plate with fish. But the flavor spectrum of wines is so infinitely wide that no chart can possibly list all of the wonderful taste-harmonies between wines and foods.

Moreover, taste is individual, so there cannot be any "wrong" wines. I happen to prefer red wine with chicken, although the charts say white is correct, and I know some winemakers who drink red wine with everything, including fish. If somewhere there exists a person who likes Cabernet Sauvignon with strawberry shortcake, he is not wrong. He is only in the minority—for himself he is right.

79

8 / Serving Ritual—
Ridiculous but Enjoyable

What Americans meekly accept from books of etiquette as rules for the correct service of wine would be amusing were it not that the existence of such rules has discouraged many people from introducing this civilized beverage into their homes. Fear of committing some error, such as using incorrect stemware or wrapping the napkin around the bottle counterclockwise when it should go the other way, has caused many a host and hostess to serve their guests palate-paralyzing highballs before dinner instead of accompanying the meal with wine, which would enhance the flavor of the food.

This becomes ridiculous as well as distressing when it is realized that the tomes of etiquette often disagree as to what is correct. Some of the rules are as garbled in translation from their commonsense Old World origins as the spelling of French dishes' names on the average American restaurant menu.

The practical solution to the questions of what constitutes proper wine service is to serve our wines as simply as we do water, coffee, soft drinks, and beer. That is how wine is served in millions of homes and restaurants in the wine countries of Europe. Bottle or carafe and glasses are placed on the table, and the host pours for the guests or lets them help themselves.

On the other hand, there is no denying that ceremony adds something to the pleasure of having wine. This is the one beverage whose rich heritage of tradition and symbolism affords the opportunity for gracious, formal service. Toasts to our guests' health can be drunk in malt or spirituous liquors, too, but only wine provides an excuse for ceremonial rites. Moreover, many of us enjoy pomp and ritual, a fact that accounts for the large memberships of many fraternal organizations.

Formal wine service can be fun, but it is no more compulsory than white tie and tails. Your unwillingness to fuss with it should not prevent you from enjoying wine.

There are in our world of connoisseurs a dozen cardinal rules of ceremonial wine service. Silly or otherwise, they are: (1) correct stemware, (2) correct table setting, (3) no smoking, (4) decanting, (5) correct wine temperatures, (6) letting red wines "breathe," (7) napkin around bottle, (8) cutting the capsule, (9) drawing the cork, (10) "pouring the cork," (11) order of service to guests, (12) correct wine with each course.

Taking them one by one, let us attempt to make sense out of these rules.

Before we consider correct stemware, I suggest that

you first get rid of those pretty sets of wineglasses you received as a wedding gift. They may look lovely displayed on a shelf, but with rare exceptions they are worse than useless for drinking wine. Why? Because the wine-ignorant manufacturers make them in thimble sizes that don't hold enough wine for more than a taste. When you serve a guest the skimpy two-ounce portion that the average one of these baubles holds, he empties it at a single sip and waits, thirsty and embarrassed, for you to pour some more.

In Europe you are served table wine in respectable stemmed bowls that would hold six, eight, nine, even twenty-two ounces if filled to the brim. They are never poured full, of course. Four or five ounces is a normal serving of table wine. The head space in the glass allows the wine to be swirled without spilling and to send forth its fragrance, which is an integral part of its taste.

You will do better to serve table wine in your water goblets, or even in your highball glasses, than in the tiny so-called wineglasses you see displayed in the housewares departments of stores. Or else buy from wine shops or specialty suppliers some of the sensible wineglasses which a few manufacturers are at last beginning to place on the market in response to the vintners' and wine hobbyists' urgent pleas. The best ones are plain in design, not colored, frosted, or cut, in order to let the wines' beautiful colors shine through. They are also tulip-shaped—narrower at the top than at the widest part of the bowl—thereby concentrating the wines' aroma and bouquet to delight your olfactory sense. I use my nine-ounce "all-purpose" glasses to

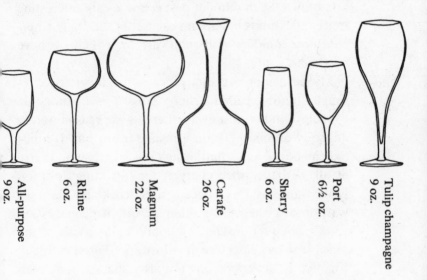

All-purpose 9 oz.

Rhine 6 oz.

Magnum 22 oz.

Carafe 26 oz.

Sherry 6 oz.

Port 6½ oz.

Tulip champagne 9 oz.

serve all types of wine, pouring them half full of table wine but less than a third full of sherry or dessert wine. Mine are also sturdy enough to survive mechanical dishwashing without breakage. Thinner ones would have to be washed and dried by hand.

Whoever first inflicted on American householders the various-sized, grotesquely shaped, colored, ornamented glasses that are sold as complete sets for the separate serving of claret, burgundy, rhine wine, sauterne, sherry, and port, must have copied them out of rare old books treasured only by glassware collectors. In Europe, it is true, each ancient winegrowing district originally developed its own distinctive wineglass. For example, the old rhine wine glasses were green to hide

83

the fact that the early white wines were often cloudy and brown. Such relics of past centuries are interesting museum exhibits but are no excuse for saddling American householders with stemware for which we have no practical use.

My particular pet annoyance is the inverted cone-shaped thimble called a sherry glass. This abominable trinket, found almost everywhere, is the reason hardly anybody orders sherry in a restaurant or bar. It holds only an ounce and a half, which is worse than no sherry at all, and the price charged for this stingy portion is the same as for a decent-sized cocktail. The outward-flaring shape is another defect; it disperses the wine's bouquet instead of confining it as does the sensible sherry glass (see the illustration) used in Spain. Finally, the inverted cone is a sissy shape; many men refuse to be seen drinking from it at all. If you happen to own a set of these ridiculous ornaments, I recommend that you either destroy them or give them to someone you especially dislike.

Despite the foregoing tirade against fancy wine-glasses, it must be admitted that our eyes condition our taste buds and that wine does taste better when sipped from an eggshell-thin, crystal-clear glass than from a kitchen tumbler or a tin cup.

The best example of eye appeal is furnished by the hollow-stemmed champagne glass. The tiny protuberance at the bottom of the hollow stem causes the wine's bubbles to cascade pleasingly upward long after the last bubbles have disappeared from the bowl. I favor the nine-ounce tulip shape, in which I serve only four ounces. The saucer-shaped champagne glass which most caterers use (which legend says was molded from the breast of Helen of Troy) has two grievous faults. It spills too readily, and it disperses both the champagne's bouquet and the bubbles, which ought to last as long as possible, tickling your nose.

The second rule of wine ritual—correct table setting—originated with the formal banquets of an earlier century. If you are serving several different wines during a dinner, there is no harm in showing how much stemware you possess. Even owning a set of the special glasses used for rhine wine makes a degree of sense, because the extra-long stem keeps the hand from warming the wine. But there is nothing wrong about using the same "all-purpose" glass for serving a whole series of wines. At each diner's right place two or three glasses (more may interfere with elbow room). Each successive wine is poured into the glass farthest to the right, which, after time for the serving of that wine is finished, is usually removed.

A number of hostesses have asked me whether to dispense with the water goblet when setting the table to include wine. Since Americans are habituated to ice water with meals, it cannot very well be omitted, but I do not fill the water glass unless the guest wishes it. In European homes there is no water glass, but a carafe of water is usually available for the guests who wish to dilute their wine.

Once at a banquet of gourmets, who regard water as fit only for bathing, I was surprised to see pitchers of that tasteless liquid standing in the center of the table. A closer look disclosed several goldfish swimming in each pitcher, an eloquent expression of the dinner committee's opinion on the subject.

Number three rule—that nobody may smoke where wine is being served—is observed only where connoisseur wine-tasting is in progress. There is plenty of smoking at banquets in the wine countries of Europe. Ashtrays are not part of the normal table setting, however; they are brought when a guest lights a cigarette.

Ritual number four, the decanting, is advisable if you are serving an old red wine that has deposited a crust of sediment on the inside of the bottle. Some of the grape solids normally settle out of a wine with the passage of years, so that sediment should be expected in a red wine of great age. (White wines, too, sometimes deposit sandlike crystals of grape tartrates, called argols.) In recent years decanting has not been needed quite as often as in the past, because modern wineries are now equipped to stabilize their wines before shipment. On the other hand, some small wineries are now making a point of neither filtering nor fining their wines and are advising customers to expect to find sediment in their bottles that should not get into a guest's glass.

If you have occasion to perform the decanting rite, the usual time to do it is just before the guests arrive. First, gently stand the crusted bottle upright long enough to let any loosened sediment settle. Then gently pour the wine from the bottle into a decanter, in front of a candle flame or flashlight. When the light discloses tiny fragments of sediment swimming by, that is the

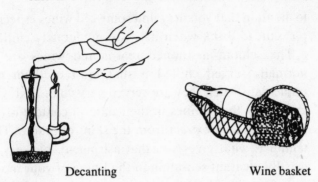

Decanting   Wine basket

point at which to stop pouring. Your guests may enjoy an opportunity to admire the empty bottle with the crust that shows the wine's age. Some hosts rinse the bottle and refill it from the decanter.

I also know some hosts who decant all red wines whether they need it or not, thereby giving their guests the impression that they are being served very old wines.

Another way to avoid putting sediment into your guests' glasses is to lay the venerable bottle on its side (with the crusted side facing down) in one of those metal cradles or wickerware wine baskets. By careful handling, the cork can be drawn almost horizontally and the wine can be poured without disturbing the crust. It is an affectation, however, to use a basket to serve a wine that is perfectly clear.

The rule nearly everybody knows about correct wine temperatures is that white, pink, and sparkling wines are always served cold but that red wines must be at "room temperature." It does not tell you *how* cold, nor at *what* room's temperature, nor why. It also fails to mention that you may find some red wines especially pleasant to drink when they are moderately chilled.

The seldom-mentioned reason red wines are not normally served chilled is that most of them taste unpleasant when they are served very cold. Red wines are higher than whites in their natural content of tannin, which they extract from the skins of grapes. Their tannin is what gives you that astringent, puckery but usually pleasant sensation in the lining of your mouth. But when a drink that is high in tannin content is served ice cold, it accentuates the puckery sensation in your mouth to an unpleasant degree. Strong tea, with extra tannin from the tea leaves, is also disagreeably extra-puckery if it is served iced.

On the other hand, the "red wine at room temperature" rule must have originated in chilly castles in England. In our overheated American homes and restaurants, this usually brings your red wine to the table lukewarm. Lukewarm wine is like lukewarm drinking water; it fails to give you the sensation of liquid; its temperature is too close to that of your mouth.

If you will do a little experimenting, you will reach the same solution most of my friends and I have: that most red wines are best-liked slightly cool (60° to 65° Fahrenheit)—which is approximately *cellar* temperature, not *room* temperature. Most whites, rosés, and champagnes are best somewhat above refrigerator temperature, or between 45° and 55°, because lower temperatures may conceal their aroma and bouquet. And any red wine that is low in tannin content—Italy's Bardolino and Valpolicella for example—can be enjoyed chilled, as we do our white wines and rosés.

In modern American homes the quickest way to chill a bottle of wine is to lay it in the freezer for a short time. If there is no hurry, a few hours in the refrigerator usually suffice. And if your red wine is too warm, a brief exposure to refrigerator or freezer will cool it to the point at which it tastes just right.

Nearly everybody nowadays is also familiar with rule six, that a red wine should be brought to the dining room an hour or more before dinner and uncorked to let it "breathe" and thus release its winy perfume. I usually advise my students to follow this custom because it is one of the pleasant bits of ritual that our guests enjoy, but not because it improves the wine or its bouquet in any way. Like many other things that are known and published about wines, the "breathing" story lacks any proof. Tests conducted by professional taste panels have shown that wines brought from the cellar and allowed to "breathe" do change slightly, not always for the better, but only because by standing in the dining room the wines become warm.

Silliest of all customs is the napkin wrapped around the bottle. Three excuses are offered for this piece of hocus-pocus: that it prevents the hand from warming a chilled bottle (in which case, why use it for red wine?); that it prevents the bottle, wet from chilling in an ice bucket, from dripping water; and that the cloth catches any drops that might drip. Actually, the napkin is only an affectation, and an unpleasant one, because it hides the label from a guest who might like to know what he is drinking. The only good excuse for the napkin

To open champagne (1) Remove top of foil cap, (2) then the wire hood, but hold your finger on the cork so it won't pop out too soon. (3) Slant the bottle *away* from your guests. Grasp the cork and twist the *bottle,* not the cork. Let internal pressure help push the cork out. (4) Hold the cork firmly as it leaves the bottle.

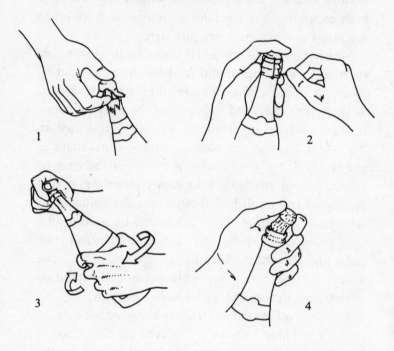

is one never mentioned: that in opening a bottle of champagne there is a one-in-a-billion chance of the bottle breaking from the pressure inside, and that the napkin protects the hand.

The best way to prevent wine from dripping on the tablecloth is to twist your wrist inward slowly as you finish pouring—thus catching any stray drops on the lip of the bottle. There also are gadgets you can buy to insert in the bottle's mouth for the same purpose.

Rule number eight—cutting the capsule—is a mere foible of people like me, who like the bottle to look its prettiest. Whereas most people tear off the foil or plastic that protects the cork or cap—thus making the bottle seem naked—the connoisseur carefully cuts it, just below the bottle's lip, before wiping the cork clean.

The next bit of ritual also makes gracious sense. It calls for the host to open the bottle at the table—not in the kitchen. There is something about the popping of the cork that whets the guests' taste for the wine. He may also display the cork to be admired, with its brand of the producer and the evidence—from how much the wine color has penetrated from the base—of how long the wine has been aged in the bottle.

Ceremony number ten is called "pouring the cork." I am often asked why this is done—that is, why the host's first action, after the bottle is opened, is to pour an ounce or two into his own glass. There are two good reasons: first, to allow him to examine and taste the wine and make certain it has not spoiled. A musty cork can make the wine smell and taste "corky." The second reason is to let any bits of broken cork go into the host's glass so that the guests will not get any.

Fussiness reaches an absurd climax in the eleventh piece of ritual: the exact order in which a wine is served to the guests. The books of etiquette are in pontifical agreement that the host must proceed counterclockwise around the table, serving first the lady at his right, then each of the other female guests, and next reverse his direction, serving wine to the gentlemen. Only a few times have I ever witnessed this solemn rite performed, and on those occasions I don't think anyone else even noticed. In other words, serve your guests in any order that is convenient.

As for the final rule, requiring the correct wine with each course, I trust that the discussion in the earlier chapter about kinds of wine for every use has already relieved the reader of any concern on that score. I do think that dry white wines taste best when served before dry reds, and the drys before the sweets. And I am not sure I agree with the connoisseur belief that the finest wine should always be served last. Our taste is probably keenest early in the meal. And does not the Bible (John 2:9–10) affirm that "every man at the beginning doth set forth the good wine," and reprove him who "hast kept the good wine until now"?

Scoring the twelve cardinal rules of wine ritual, then—here is how we stand. The correct wineglass to use is a glass that is big enough to supply a decent serving and to allow the wine to be swirled. The rigid rules of table setting, no smoking, letting red wines "breathe," napkin around bottle, capsule-cutting, cork-drawing, pouring and serving, and correct wine with each course, can all be safely ignored. Chill all white, rosé, and sparkling wines; the rest should be served the way they taste best to you. And the napkin around the bottle should be abolished.

Finally, here is the secret of how to open corked bottles with a flourish instead of a struggle. Of course, if you use only wines sealed with the easily opened

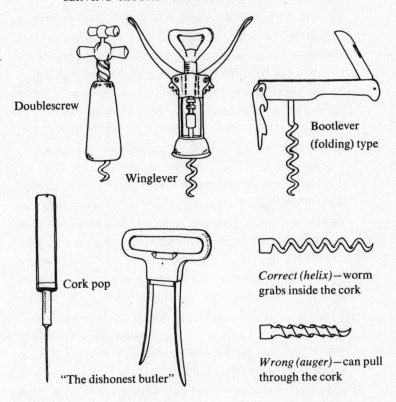

Doublescrew

Winglever

Bootlever
(folding) type

Cork pop

"The dishonest butler"

Correct (helix)—worm grabs inside the cork

Wrong (auger)—can pull through the cork

Bottle Openers To pull corks with a flourish, use a corkscrew that has leverage. Three kinds with leverage are pictured. Be sure your corkscrew has an efficient 2-inch-long worm (the business part that goes into the cork) and insert it all the way. Sketches show right and wrong kinds of worms. The wrong kind has its point in the center; it drills a hole in the cork and can pull right through. With the "cork pop" opener, you poke the hollow needle through the cork and pump air into the bottle, making the cork pop out. To use "the dishonest butler," insert one knife-like prong on each *side* of the cork with a rocking motion, then lift with a gradual twist. The cork can be replaced undetected, giving this gadget its name.

screw caps, you don't need this advice. But since most higher-priced wines are closed by long, straight, often stubborn corks, it is quite necessary. If you have ever suffered the ignominy of straining vainly to pull a cork with the bottle held between your knees—or of being compelled to push the pesky plug into the bottle with a pencil because the corkscrew had pulled completely through—you will especially value the following suggestion.

This is to go shopping for a good cork-remover. There are many gadgets that are performing the bottle-opening function admirably. The way they work is made clear, I hope, in the sketches and the captions.

But the traditional method is to use a corkscrew. That implement must have two distinct virtues: good leverage and a good worm. Corkscrews on the market come with several different kinds of leverage—some quite elaborate, but all of them good. Don't let these shiny appendages hypnotize you into buying a corkscrew with an inefficient worm.

In fact, the worm—the part that goes into the cork and mustn't let go—is by far the most important part. The point of the worm must be exactly in line with its spirals; there should be an open space down the center. The worm should also be long enough to go all the way through a two-inch-long cork; and the edges should not be sharp. Never buy a corkscrew whose point is exactly in the center; if you own one of those, throw it away before it fails you, because it eventually will.

You can safely take my word for the foregoing,

because in 1944 I launched a two-year Wine Institute corkscrew research project, enlisting the aid of the world-famous physicist, Dr. Leonard B. Loeb. We tested every known shape of corkscrew and finally revealed the previously undiscovered mechanical principle involved. It is so simple that we should not have needed the tests to discover it. A sharp-edged worm with its point centered is actually an auger; it bores a hole and weakens the cork. But a worm with point and spirals in perfect alignment, and with no sharp edges, worms its way into the cork without weakening it; and when it is pulled, grips the cork from the inside and doesn't let go.

As a result of our tests dozens of manufacturers redesigned their corkscrews to conform to the foregoing specifications. However, unfortunately, not all have done so—which is why the corkscrew buyer must still beware.

9 / The Great Restaurant Swindle

Someday in the not too distant future we who enjoy wine with our meals will be able to have it served to us in the average American hotel and restaurant without being victimized by extortionate prices.

I can also state that the time is fast approaching when our wine will be served to us unspoiled, chilled or unchilled as it should be, as promptly as any other item on the menu, and at prices close to what good wine is worth.

The reason I confidently make these statements is that a few of our restaurateurs are already beginning to realize that they have long been swindling their patrons with badly served, overpriced wines and that by so doing they have also been cheating themselves. What has begun to awaken them is the spectacular trebling of mealtime wine consumption in American homes during the past decade and the sobering fact that the restaurant industry has thus far failed to win its share of the wine-sales boom.

96

One sign of the awakening is that for the first time since the repeal of Prohibition, it now is actually possible to order wine by the glass and by the carafe in restaurants, hotels, and clubs throughout the United States. With rare exceptions, however, the glass and carafe of wine being sold are exorbitantly priced and therefore are only occasionally bought.

From a gallon jug of one-year-old California chablis, rosé, or burgundy costing two to five dollars at wholesale, a restaurant can serve twenty-five five-ounce glasses with only a fourth of the effort and tableware involved in serving coffee in a cup with saucer, cream, sugar, and spoon. Yet a check of restaurant menus and wine lists I made in two dozen cities during 1974 showed the prices being charged for such wines ranged from fifty cents to a dollar and a half a glass. Since the cost of the wine to the restaurant ranged from two cents to at most four cents an ounce, amounting to only ten to twenty cents per five-ounce glass, the restaurants were reaping gross profits of from 250 to 900 percent.

At the same time, a bottle of everyday French, Italian, Spanish, or California wine was costing the average restaurant less than two dollars, sometimes considerably less. My examination of prices showed that restaurants in such cities as New York, Chicago, Detroit, Miami, San Francisco, and Los Angeles were charging credulous patrons four to ten dollars for these same bottles—two to five times what they cost the proprietors. Obviously the improvement has only begun.

97

Why has this continued? Because we, the public, have not yet learned to complain about the wine swindle, though we do complain when our soup is served lukewarm or the ice cream comes to the table melted. I sometimes wonder whether people pay exorbitant prices for wine in restaurants because they actually enjoy paying more than it is worth. How else to explain it, when they see the same wines offered for less than half as much around the corner at the store? The swindle continues also because American restaurateurs are mainly a stubborn lot, given to aping one another, unwilling to experiment with innovations in merchandising and unable to see that they easily could sell ten times as much wine as their present volume if their avarice were not beclouding their business sense. They have not realized that not only their wine sales, but their total patronage will grow when their food becomes better appreciated with the flavor-enhancing accompaniment of good wine. Until they do, most of their customers will continue drinking ice water, on which the restaurant not only makes no profit, but suffers a loss.

I am finding some improvement in pricing in the new kind of restaurant called a wine bar, which offers wine tasting and features the sale of wine by the glass with snacks and cheese. The proprietors of these places profit not only from their sales of wine in a generous glass at fifty to sixty cents, but the wines they serve are so good that their patrons also buy them by the case to take home.

There also is improvement in some of our smaller

cities, where new restaurateurs who start by knowing nothing about wine take up its study and soon develop better wine assortments and service than are found in the big city establishments whose proprietors are too old to learn. I have often found better wine lists and more nearly reasonable wine prices in suburban and country town restaurants than in the big cities' downtown restaurants and hotels.

What is a fair profit for restaurants on wine? Retail stores generally sell their fast-moving advertised brands at markups of a third to at most a half over their per-bottle cost. A textbook on restaurant hotel accounting recommends that such establishments' total revenues from foods and beverages should average five times their cost. This is equivalent to requiring a standard markup of four hundred per cent over cost. By this formula, the restaurant that buys champagne from a wholesaler at three dollars a bottle would be correct in trying to charge you fifteen dollars!

A restaurant is obviously entitled to a higher markup than a retail store because of the cost of service and stemware. But food is something the restaurant has created from raw materials, while wine is produced by the winegrower and comes to the restaurant ready to be opened and served.

A professor of hotel management in Michigan once suggested to me that a reasonable charge for a bottle of wine in a restaurant might be the retail store price plus a half dollar to perhaps a dollar for service. For a California wine selling at three dollars in retail stores in states where laws require the posting of prices, this would let the restaurant sell the wine at up to four dollars. Since the wholesale price was two dollars, this would be a restaurant markup of one hundred percent over its cost. If the professor's formula were to be adopted, wine prices in restaurants would be considerably less than they are now.

One of the causes of the present excessive markups is that restaurant accountants have not yet recognized that wine, unlike hard liquor which is a bar item, is part of a meal and is served by personnel who work out of the kitchen. If restaurants would only transfer their wine accounting from their bar to their food operations, their wine prices would decline at least to some extent.

When the bright future of wine in United States eating places eventually arrives, it will bring several improvements in addition to fair wine prices. For one thing, wines will come to our tables in improved condition. At present, because not enough restaurant personnel have been taught that table wines are perishable, wines are kept too long in overheated storerooms and also too long standing up in refrigerators. The need is to train the personnel that wine stocks must be rotated, that bottles stored longest in unfavorable temperatures should be sold before those newly delivered to the restaurant. The failure to rotate wine stocks is the reason I have often been served white wines so oxidized that they had begun to taste like sherry.

Service eventually will improve with increased wine sales, too. One reason many patrons do not order wines is the restaurants' reliance for wine-selling on the single wine waiter costumed with chain, key, and tasting cup as a wine steward or *sommelier*. Some of these haughty individuals intimidate patrons with a stare when a wine name is mispronounced or when they receive an order for a moderately priced wine. I have known some *sommeliers* so inflated with their importance that they actually taste a wine before pouring any for the patron to taste.

There is a solution to the problem of slow wine service. The secret is to start, the moment you reach your table, a relentless campaign to get your wine served in time. Immediately you are seated, ask for the wine list. If none is to be had, confer with the captain or bartender to learn what wines he has in stock. Make your selection, and request that the wine be brought to your table immediately. By making the request early you may, if you are lucky, get it served in time to drink with your main course. For a waiter's acceptance of your wine order does not mean it will be delivered. Instead, he may return with your food ready to be eaten, and report with a smirk that the establishment is freshly out of the wine you ordered. This used to happen to me so frequently that I now make it a rule not to even order my dinner before my wine has arrived.

Resist all attempts to foist expensive wines on you and to make you feel cheap when you order a moderately priced bottle. The fact is that restaurant people despise the sucker who yields to their salesmanship

101

in behalf of overpriced imports. They secretly respect the seasoned patron who orders the best wine bargain in the house.

If you are served a corky or an oxidized wine, do not hesitate to send it back and insist on its replacement with a sound bottle. Any restaurant waiter, captain, maître d', or manager who cannot recognize a corky or an oxidized wine is either taste blind or knows nothing about wines.

The unpredictability of restaurant food quality in recent years has brought about the publication of periodical private guides to restaurants which perform a valuable service except that when they praise a restaurant too highly, it soon becomes overcrowded with new patrons. A defect of the private guides is that they rate restaurants primarily by food and service and ignore how the restaurant handles wines. It seems to me that if we would begin rating restaurants first by their wines, especially by the quality and reasonable prices of their "house wines" or carafe wines, this would also be the best guide to the quality of their food. For where a good carafe wine is lacking in a restaurant, something is wrong; and where there is fine wine that reflects the restaurateur's good taste in drink to accompany his fare, there is always fine food.

The public eventually gets what it wants in products and service, as witness the revolutionary recent changes in stores and automobiles. Our restaurateurs cannot continue for many more years to ignore the growing demand for wine with food. We lovers of wine will eventually have our way.

10 / What Vintners Don't Tell

My winegrower friends often mildly wonder at the naiveté of fascinated outsiders who write admiring books and articles about the vintner's art. To those who labor in vineyard and cellar, the growing of grapes and the fermenting of the juice into wine seem essentially simple operations. Mother Nature, after all, does the principal work. Art and science are employed only to assure that Nature will do it well— that the liquid will not spoil (as it would if left untended), that the finished product will be clear, not cloudy, and that it will be as fragrant and delicious as circumstances permit.

Some of the popular misconceptions about wine, although they enhance its charm, are partly responsible for its as yet limited use in the United States. Vintners, reluctant to dispel their customers' romantic illusions, make little or no effort to correct them. In this respect the vintner resembles the old man in the story who, charged with seducing a lovely young woman, found the accusation so flattering that he could not resist pleading guilty.

103

THE MYTH OF OLD WINE

The purpose of this chapter is to straighten out a few of the more prevalent warped impressions. One of these is the myth of old wine.

Almost everyone regards great age as the noblest of all vinous virtues. Poets pen verses in praise of venerable vintages, and thereby help to perpetuate the fallacy that wines must be old to be good.

Yet most of the world's wine is consumed before it is even a year old. It is well that this is so, because the average wine, if stored for many years, is more likely to lose quality than to improve. Most rosés, for example, are at their peak of delicious drinking quality at the moment they leave the winery and until about six months of age. After that point they begin losing their fresh aroma and flavor, commence to turn brown and to taste that way. White table wines, with a few exceptions, are also likely to attain their optimum taste and fragrance within a year after vintage. The same is true of many reds.

People need to know this, because the really important wines for America are the young, wholesome, inexpensive table wines that can fit in the average household budget for daily use with meals. These are the wines that have begun at long last to civilize drinking in this country.

Far be it from me to deny the marvelous improvement in mellowness, complex flavor, and bouquet that aging accomplishes in exceptional wines. It is their ability to gain quality with age that makes them exceptional. It also makes them expensive works of art, because they are produced from only the costliest grapes, and each additional year they are aged at the winery further multiplies their cost. Old wines, if they are fine, are intended to be sipped and revered. Young, everyday wines are to be drunk and enjoyed.

In past years the myth of old wine was so firmly fixed in the public mind that vintners did everything they could to encourage the impression that all their wines were old. Lately this has begun to change, partly perhaps because of the Beaujolais craze in France.

On November 15 of each year, the new red wine of Beaujolais in southern Burgundy, made from grapes harvested during September, is shipped to Paris and London to be drunk before Christmas. Lines of trucks form outside the wineries the day before because French law does not allow the shipments to leave until a minute after midnight. To emphasize its youth and that it is freshly bottled, the wine is labeled *primeur* (early, fresh) or *nouveau* (new).

The fad for weeks-old red wine has spread to this country. Now, in late November, some California wineries are shipping wines labeled Gamay Beaujolais *nouveau* or Merlot *primeur,* made from grapes picked in October, to reach cities across the country before the new Beaujolais arrives from France.

Some of the labels proclaim a new way of quickly fermenting the whole, uncrushed grapes, called carbonic maceration (which isn't new; it's really ancient).

105

Recent advances in wine technology have contributed much newer methods of getting sound wines onto the market in weeks instead of months or years.

SPOILAGE IS BY DEGREES

Rather than belittle the delightful quality of old wines, I devote much of the later chapter on wine cellars to the choosing and care of those rare bottles that improve with the passage of years. But it is important to let people know that most wines have only a brief life span, that each matures at a different time and thereafter fades. In America, where many purveyors are still innocent of wine knowledge, tens of thousands of bottles, especially of white and rosé table wines, are being allowed to spoil in stores and restaurants before they are sold. This also happens in Europe, where some of the cobwebbed bottles in restaurants' wine cellars are long past their prime.

Spoilage of wine is only a matter of degree. Spoiled wines have only lost quality; they are still entirely safe and not necessarily unpleasant to drink. What is meant nowadays by wine spoilage can be appreciated by visualizing a perfect peach freshly picked from the tree and a perfectly fresh, crisp head of lettuce. If they were left to stand in a warm room for a few days, you know what would happen; dark spots would appear on the peach and the merest touch would rub off patches of its once perfect skin. Both peach and lettuce would have deteriorated, become tired, no longer good.

In earlier days, spoiled wine meant wine that had

begun to turn to vinegar. This rarely happens nowadays, and mainly in inexpertly homemade wine. Vinegar fermentation in sound commercial wine has been virtually eliminated by modern winemaking, especially by sterile microfiltration.

The principal kind of spoilage now is oxidation—exposure to air, light, or heat. These oxidize the wine, much as oxygen rusts iron. The wine begins to taste somewhat like sherry, a wine which is oxidized on purpose. When a perfect table wine or champagne begins to become oxidized, it has deteriorated, lost some of its quality, just like the tired peach and lettuce. If the bottle of wine was worth five dollars when it was perfect, oxidation has reduced its value to perhaps fifty cents.

Much the same kind of partial spoilage occurs when a wine gradually becomes too old, when we say it has gone over the hill. But it is tragic to let it happen, as so unfortunately it often does, to a wine that could still have been perfect had it been properly stored.

WHAT DATES REALLY MEAN

The only way you can determine a wine's age is to look for a vintage year statement, if any, on the label and perform a little arithmetic. Why not simply state the number of years of age, as whisky labels do? A government regulation prohibits it, and vintners approve of this taboo. Mere age is deceptive as an index of wine quality because some wines lose quality while some fine wines improve. Wine differs entirely from liquor, which does not change after it is bottled. A whisky which was five years old when it left the barrel will still be five years old twenty years later.

Vintage dates are a prolific source of wine confusion. In European countries the vintage year statement is used to identify the occasional years when the weather in the vineyard districts has been sunny enough to fully ripen the grapes. Years of bad weather, and of consequently poor wines, occur in these countries with such unpleasant frequency that the connoisseur finds it necessary to learn which are the good years, simply to avoid buying the bad. This makes it necessary for the buyer of old wines to carry in his wallet, as I do, one of the vintage cards printed by the importing firms. The cards list the recent years in which each European region produced wines that the importer considers good, fair, or poor.

In California, the source of most American wines, the long, rainless summers permit the grapes to mature every year, even in the occasional years when the vineyards experience periods of autumn rains. It is often said that every year is a vintage year in California, although those who make the statement concede that the state's wines do change with the weather from year to year. But the purpose of vintage dates on European wines, to identify the poor years, does not apply here.

Many wineries refuse to use the vintage labels at all. With large reserve stocks, they can blend together wines of different ages, adding the freshness and aroma of the young to the mellowness, complexity, and fra-

108

grance of the old. Such blending also enables them to maintain year-to-year uniformity in the flavor of each type of wine they sell. There are no vintage labels on Spanish sherries or on other fine wines of the oxidized types, because their chief virtue is their fractional-blending or *solera* system, by which the youngest wines are continuously blended with older and with the very oldest wines.

A major objection to vintage dating is that the United States labeling regulation requires, when a year is stated, that 95 percent of the wine in the bottle must have been grown and fermented during that year. The remaining five percent is an allowance for topping (refilling) the casks to replace wine that has been lost by evaporation. This is necessary to protect the remaining wine from being injured by exposure to air. But while the 95 percent rule is strictly enforced in the United States, our government has no inspectors watching what happens in wineries in other countries. Germany requires 75 percent of a vintage-labeled wine to be of the year stated, but elsewhere there is nothing except the foreign vintner's conscience to prevent him from stretching a good vintage with a bad.

Vintage dates on American wines are useful mainly in identifying the varying batches or casks bottled by the small premium wineries, and especially in telling you the age of a bottle that you lay down for aging in your cellar. But the fact that a wine has a vintage date does not mean that it is better than one without. Since vintage labels have become associated in buyers' minds with premium quality wines, some marketers of everyday wines have begun labeling their wines, too, with vintage dates.

A wine-store proprietor once commented on this subject as follows: "Vintages, schmintages!" he said. "To me they're just a lot of numbers. My customers keep telling me I have the right wine but the wrong vintage. What I want to know is, why do the wineries insist on making their stuff so complicated?" His complaint is largely justified, because a vintage date is not a sound guide to wine satisfaction; and some of the best wines are undated.

PUZZLE OF THOSE BOTTLE SHAPES

Let us now discuss another puzzling subject that vintners find it hard to explain—the shapes of their bottles. Why must certain wine types, both white and red, come only in the narrow-shouldered, broad-based burgundy bottle? Why the broad-shouldered, straight-sided Bordeaux shape; the tall, slender hock bottle; the straight-necked, narrow-waisted one for dessert wines, and the other still odder shapes?

The answer is that wine bottle shapes are a matter of tradition that, like many other traditions, does not quite fit our present ways. Wines named burgundy and chablis (the latter named for a village in northern Burgundy) traditionally must come in the burgundy bottle. So must Chardonnay and Pinot Noir, since the grapes are Burgundian varieties. A wine labeled claret, a Bordeaux type, uses the Bordeaux bottle, and so must the Cabernets, Sémillons, and Sauvignon Blanc, although the latter is also a Loire Valley grape and has

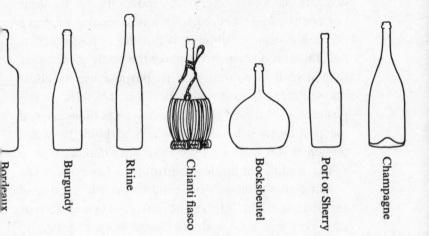

Bordeaux　　Burgundy　　Rhine　　Chianti fiasco　　Bocksbeutel　　Port or Sherry　　Champagne

three different names there. Zinfandel, which is unknown in France, also must use the Bordeaux bottle, because vintners say it resembles claret more than it does burgundy. The several Rieslings, being mostly German grapes, use the hock bottle (named for Hochheim in the Rheingau), but you also often find rosés in this German bottle shape, which at least reminds you to serve them cold. Chilean vintners have adopted the stubby bocksbeutel, which originally was used only for the Steinweins of Franconia; and the makers of most Portuguese rosés now use it, too. The Italian vintners, however, are unhappy with their classic chianti *fiasco*, because its handwoven straw cover now costs more than the wine it contains. They are trying to substitute a plastic replica of the straw.

As for the pushup (also called the punt, or kick) in the base of some bottles, authorities on its history disagree as to its original purpose. There are four current theories: one, that it was intended to make the bottle strong, although it has the opposite effect; two, that it was intended to make the bottle seem larger than it really is; three, that its purpose was to allow the sediment in wine to collect on the sides of the pushup; and finally, that early-day glass blowers used the pushup as a handle by which to hold the semi-molten bottle with a glove. Take your choice.

The traditional bottles contribute at least one value —their colors. Europe's old-time vintners learned long ago that sunlight injures the flavor of wine. That is why they use mostly dark-colored bottles, generally brown or green, but a special pale green for moselles. Some vintners, however, now bottle their products in clear glass to let the consumer see what he is buying, even though this endangers quality, and ultraviolet rays destroy some of the vitamins in wine.

I am happy to report that this matter of protecting wines from light has not revived the post-Prohibition attempt to popularize wine in cans, which threatened to strip away some of the romance. Vintners in Europe, however, have done something else. They have introduced table wines in transparent plastic bottles, which our government has barred from this country because of a rumor that the plastic might react with the wine. In France they now also sell table wines in cardboard cartons such as those we use for milk, the difference being that the cartons have a metallic lining that is impervious to the acids in wine. Most wine in

112

Europe is sold in returnable bottles, returnable jugs, and in barrels, from which the householder bottles the wine himself.

CORKS VERSUS SCREW CAPS

The subject of bottle closures is equally confused.

When the repeal of Prohibition revived the wine industry in 1933, few American households owned good corkscrews, and many of the reopened wineries adopted the easy-to-open screw cap as the closure for their wines. The older premium wineries, however, continued using the old-fashioned straight corks, which are imported from Spain and Portugal; and the European wines came as in the past with their traditional corks.

A controversy ensued as to which closure better protects wine. The advocates of corks claimed that a wine needs to "breathe" through the cork. The screw cap proponents replied that corks do not breathe, that they only leak. The supporters of corks then attacked the screw cap on the ground that it seals only the lip of the bottle and that the metal of the cap eventually tires and admits air, while the cork seals for its entire length inside the bottle neck. Still another argument was that the headspace between a wine and a screw cap is greater than that between wine and cork, thus exposing the wine to more air inside the bottle when the cap is used.

Now the subject of closures, still unsettled, has become further confused. Because many people have

113

become accustomed to paying higher prices for premium and imported wines that are closed with corks, some vintners who formerly used only screw caps have begun using corks and have raised their prices as well.

In the middle of the closure controversy is the plastic "cork" for champagne. Made in the same size as the thick, seven-piece laminated champagne cork, the plastic plug is now used by some champagne producers because it is easier than the cork to remove. However, plastic does not expand as natural cork does, and as the insides of champagne bottles may vary slightly in diameter, the gas may escape, leaving the champagne flat.

There are some more things worth noticing about corks, such as the way they vary in quality and in length. Vintners who expect you to age their wines in the bottle for many years may use the costly two-inch-long corks. Others, who know that some of their customers own faulty corkscrews, may settle for the inch-and-three-quarters size, which also costs them less.

But the most important fact to know about corks is that if you ever are served a wine that smells and tastes musty, which happens to me every year or two, you should not immediately blame the winery, because the cause may be a bad cork. Cork is a vegetable substance, the bark of a cork oak tree, and sometimes a fungus begins to grow in the material and cannot be detected by the winery. The result is that you are served a corky wine, which you should return to be replaced.

IT SHOULD COST LESS THAN MILK

Another subject which vintners seldom discuss in public is their cost of production, especially in comparison with the prices we consumers pay for wines.

The blunt fact, which I have already stated, is that wine is actually cheaper to produce than milk. One recent comparison showed that one gallon of milk freshly pumped from the cow costs the average dairyman nearly as much as two gallons of sound new wine, made of standard grape varieties, are likely to cost the average winery.

In addition are the costs of bottle, cork or screw cap, label, case, and transportation. But even these, plus the profits of distributors and retailers, fall far short of accounting for the wine prices in average American stores.

The point I am making is that the federal and state gallonage taxes on wine (the only article of food that is so taxed) are in some cases several times greater than the value of the product. The federal tax alone, during 1974, was equivalent to $275 for an acre of grape land producing table wine, or $650 if the land was used for dessert wine.

One reason vintners rarely discuss this subject in public is that other alcoholic beverages nowadays are taxed even more; and the winegrowers, in a nation which still fails to distinguish this wholesome drink from hard liquor, understandably refrain from even raising the issue.

But wine, unlike beer and distilled spirits, is primarily an article of food. To those of us who use it daily on our family dinner tables it is an integral part of our diet like bread and meat. Wine is not something manufactured but is a product of the soil, a fruit juice fermented by the farmer at the vineyard.

It is up to the consuming public, rather than to the vintners, to demand of our federal and state legislators relief from these exorbitant taxes. For the vintner does not pay them; he merely advances the money, and in the final analysis we consumers pay these taxes every time we buy a bottle of wine.

In Spain, where wine is recognized as food, it is subject to no excise tax whatever. A bottle of ordinary table wine costs the householder less than an equal quantity of beer or even of a bottle of drinking water.

But the most amazing comparison between the value of a wine and the tax it pays is furnished by champagne. In 1974 the federal tax on this sparkling wine was $3.40 per gallon—twenty times the tax on table wine. This is something about which vintners *do* complain.

It might be argued that champagne, unlike everyday burgundy and chablis, is a luxury—the beverage for celebrating special occasions such as weddings—and should be taxed as such.

But the fact is that an average champagne is really little more than a rather neutral white table wine, which you probably could not distinguish from chablis if it didn't contain bubbles. There is a widespread belief, obviously shared by the Congress, that this effervescent drink is one of the most intoxicating of all beverages.

Yet, unless bubbles in wine can make you giddy—which has been conclusively disproved in tests—any such effect must be purely psychological, because champagne contains no more alcohol than many white table wines. The bubbles are merely the same carbon dioxide that makes soda pop sparkle.

Granted, there is also something special about the extra-thick champagne bottle and its massive wired-in cork, which makes the jolly popping noise if you let it fly toward the ceiling (which you shouldn't, by the way, because it can injure someone). These, too, are purely ornamental, because the champagne would be equally safe in a modern crown-capped coke bottle. In other words, the government is taxing us, the public, all of those extra dollars for nothing but the bubbles.

Even more extortionate is the $2.40 per gallon federal tax on artificially carbonated wine, which is not allowed to call itself champagne or even to be labeled "sparkling." The government is not entirely to blame for this imposition on a public that likes effervescent drinks. The producers of champagne, fearing that bartenders preparing champagne cocktails might substitute carbonated wine for the genuine product, have insisted that the tax on this potential competitor be kept high.

Equally unjustified is the collection of the full champagne tax rate on the product called crackling wine, which is champagne in which the pressure is weak and the bubbles are few.

There has been a lengthy controversy on this subject of bubbles in wine. In 1958 it was partly resolved with the Congress voted to allow "still" wines to contain carbon dioxide up to about seven pounds per square inch pressure without being subject to increased taxes; and in 1974 it was raised to a full "atmosphere," about 14.7 pounds. These wines, which thus far have been principally of the flavored and fancifully named "pop" types, may not be labeled or represented as effervescent, because if they were, the fourteen-times-higher tax on carbonated wine would apply.

TRUTH ABOUT "ADDITIVES"

Something else you seldom hear mentioned by vintners is the "finishing" their products receive, but this is often being mentioned nowadays by consumer advocates who know nothing about wine. They claim that wines are being treated by a long list of chemical additives specifically permitted by the government. There is a grain of truth in the claim, but the impression created is completely false. Wine for sale in the United States is the natural product of sound, ripe grapes "without other addition or abstraction except as may occur in cellar treatment," according to the federal regulations, which are the strictest in the world. Cellar treatment necessary to prevent wine from clouding or spoiling has been practiced for at least five thousand years. The government prescribes the permissible addition of a list of seventy-one substances, many of them duplicated under different names, which are naturally present in grapes, such as yeasts, enzymes, sulfur dioxide, and fruit acids, and also materials that may be used to fine (clarify) wines, but which settle to the bottom of a cask from which the clear wine is drawn off. With rare exceptions, nothing that is not a natural constituent of grapes remains in the wine.

One reason the list is long is that Americans have never learned to accept sediment in wines. The need to keep sediment out of the bottles also accounts for much of the shiny equipment you see inside modern wineries. Most of it has nothing to do with making wine, but is there primarily to filter, polish, and stabilize the liquid—to make it look and stay looking attractive. One of the methods is to chill new wines, causing the dissolved or suspended grape solids to deposit in the cask so that they will not do so in the bottle.

Some connoisseurs like to display their vinous knowledge by denouncing all modern processing, and they especially disapprove of pasteurized wines. Here they reach a ridiculous extreme, for pasteurization is merely the same protection given to prevent spoilage in milk. Nobody has ever proved that a wine, properly pasteurized, tastes at all different from one not so protected.

Actually, while vintners treasure the romance and traditions of their ancient art and try to make their advertisements exude the atmosphere of moss-covered caves and wooden casks, grape and wine technology has advanced more since the Second World War than in the preceding two thousand years. Science has taken the guesswork out of winemaking. America and Germany have led the advances, which account for the vastly improved taste and reliability of their wines. The lead in research has been taken by the University of California, which now attracts students from all parts of the world to its wine school at Davis. Important contributions have also been made by the New York State Agricultural Experiment Station at Geneva, and since the dramatic rise in wine consumption began in the 1960s, wine research activity has spread to universities and colleges in at least a dozen other states.

RETURN OF THE OAK BARREL

One of the most noticeable changes brought about by research has been the appearance of stainless-steel and epoxy-lined steel tanks for wine, replacing the old-fashioned big wooden and concrete tanks. It has been found that some wines taste better and are more fragrant if they are never allowed to touch wood during aging.

This, of course, sounds like heresy, for the traditional wooden cask is the romantic symbol of old wine. But how did wood come to be used for wine storage in the first place? The original wine containers of the ancients were earthenware jars called amphorae, with pointed bases which were stuck into the earth to hold them upright. Wood came into use much later, as a substitute capable of being built to hold large quantities for mass production.

But while steel is fast replacing the largest old wooden casks, the trend is also operating in reverse. More small oak barrels have lately come into use in American wineries than ever before. This is because the vintners have learned that certain of the very finest wines require some oak taste. A wine aged in an oak barrel extracts aromatic substances from the wood which combine with the tastes contributed by grapes and help produce the elusive quality called complexity in the flavor and bouquet of the wine. Vintners have also learned that there are many kinds of oak, which have their own distinctive varietal flavors. In particular, some wines are at their best when aged in American white oak, while others require the taste of the different oak varieties that grow on the European continent—which are not found in North American forests.

WHY PRICES GO UP AND DOWN

Finally, let us discuss why wine prices fluctuate from year to year as sharply as they do. The law of supply and demand is the reason, of course. It applies more to wine than to any of the other alcoholic beverages because wine is a product grown on the farm like vegetables, fruits, and other foods. A succession of years of sunny weather, bringing a succession of bumper grape crops, can cause a wine surplus, and prices then may dip. On the other hand, years of disastrous spring frosts can reduce the grape crop, causing wine shortages and sending prices steeply up. This may cause farmers to plant more vines, which begin to bear crops in three to four years; and if too many are planted, this can cause another glut of the wine market, and lower prices again.

Wine quality may also vary with fluctuations in the supply of grapes and in the prices of wines. Temporarily high grape prices may tempt a grape grower to

121

overcrop his vines, causing a loss in the quality of the resulting wine, or a vintner may yield to the temptation to stretch his fine wine with cheaper grapes. The point all this leads to is that the vintner who consistently receives high prices for his wine is thereby motivated not to let his quality decline. When you have reason to believe that he is doing his best, you should be willing to pay the prices he asks for his finest wines.

11 / Some Labels Unriddled

If the vintners of the world had united in a mischievous effort to confuse the buyers of their products, they could scarcely have succeeded better than they have done without even trying. Surely there is no other widely used food or beverage whose bottles, cans, or boxes have more confusing labels than those on bottles of wine.

In the Key to 362 Wines I have listed the principal wines available in North America and described how the liquids under the corks are likely to taste. Now I shall try to unriddle some of the mystifying type names, flavor terms, alcohol contents, medals, estates, *crus*, grape names, and what—if anything—geographic designations mean.

HOW DRY IS "DRY"?

Let me start with the terms vintners use to describe degrees of product sweetness: "dry," "extra dry," *"sec,"* *"brut,"* "natural," *"doux,"* "cream," and *"haut."* Here we have an example of what semanticist S. I. Haya-kawa, the author of *Language in Thought and Action,* meant when he wrote: "The writer of a dictionary is a historian, not a lawgiver." Dictionaries, Hayakawa contends, merely record what words have meant in the distant or immediate past—not what they mean today. For only one of the eight terms supposed to designate degrees of wine sweetness actually means precisely what it says.

If the following explanation happens to inspire some hilarity, please remember that it is intended to be purely serious and factual.

There can be little doubt that the original sherries and champagnes—generations ago—were sweet. But it seems that certain high-placed connoisseurs in England objected to the sweet taste, demanded wines made dry, and were accommodated with "dry" sherry and *"sec"* champagne. ("Dry" meant nonsweet; *"sec"* meant the same in French.)

Soon—as the story goes—the wine snobs of that era, noting that people with prestige as connoisseurs drank only the "dry" and *"sec"* wines, began insisting on having their wines so labeled, too. But most people, then as now, prefer wines that taste somewhat sweet; and the vintners of that early era soon discovered the way to prosperity. They simply made the wines sweet but labeled them dry.

When the connoisseurs began to complain that their "dry" and *"sec"* wines were no longer dry, the vintners again obliged—by finding new words for the labels. They came up with "extra-dry" for genuinely dry sherry, and unsweetened champagne became *"brut"* (French for "rough," "raw," or "unadulterated").

But soon the cycle was repeated: fashion-conscious Britons demanded wines with the "extra-dry" and *"brut"* labels—and these gradually became sweet, too. So now we have "bone-dry" sherries and "natural" or *"naturel"* champagne—while "dry," "extra-dry," *"sec,"* and *"brut"* wines are gradually becoming sweeter.

How long it will be before the snobs prevail once more—and vintners will need to find still more words that mean nonsweet—is anybody's guess.

Meanwhile, many Americans are saying: "I only like wines that are dry," imagining that the word means "high quality." Of course they are only fooling themselves, because when they do taste a dry wine, they complain that it tastes "sour." (A really sour wine is a spoiled wine; it has refermented, forming acetic acid and beginning to turn into vinegar.)

Moreover, the rape of "dry" as a descriptive term for beverages is now complete, because a "dry" martini cocktail has come to mean only that the once-mandatory ingredient—vermouth—is now administered with an atomizer; and most of today's martini drinkers are sipping virtually straight gin.

I said there is one wine-sweetness term which actually means what it says. That is *"doux,"* which means "sweet" in French. French champagne producers once did sell a little of this honestly labeled product in Russia, but they find little sale for it in the United States. In this country, perhaps because of the national

125

concern over calories, "sweet" in any language somehow seems to be a naughty word. Consequently, an extra-sweet champagne, in order to sell to Americans, has to be labeled—of all things—*"demi-sec"* or "semi-dry."

"CREAM," "DEMI-SEC," "DOUX," AND "HAUT"

This is also why the sweetest sherries are labeled "cream sherry."

The demand for wines with "dry" labels even fools some vintners. They make truly dry wines and never quite understand why their sales are so disappointing.

At any rate, you can be assured from the foregoing paragraphs that "bone-dry" sherries and "natural" champagnes are likely to be quite dry—at least for the time being—and that "cream" sherries and *"demi-sec"* and *"doux"* champagnes will surely be very sweet. As for the rest, while you know that "dry" is theoretically sweeter than "extra-dry" and that *"sec"* should be sweeter than *"brut,"* you cannot be sure of how dry or sweet the individual wine so designated will be, until you first learn what the individual vintner means by his label.

Officials who deal with wines in Canada have given up trying to use words to describe dryness or sweetness. They have devised a numbering system instead. Each wine sold in Canadian wine stores now has a number between 0 (for dry) and 10 (sweet).

This brings us to the strange story of "haut sauterne."

In France, where sauternes originated around the Bordeaux village of Sauternes, this type of white wine

126

is always semi-sweet. In America, most sauterne is quite dry. In order to supply a sauterne as sweet as the French one—but to avoid labeling it sweet—American vintners adopted another French term. They call it "haut sauterne."

But while visiting in France years ago I was told emphatically there was no such French wine as "haut sauterne." And I have a letter in my files from the Institut National des Appellations d'Origine des Vins et Eaux-de-Vie, repeating that denial. It reads, in part:

"Concerning Haut-Sauterne, we have no idea how it came to be used. There is no such name in France, only Sauternes, name of a village and of a wine produced in the delimited area around this village. Haut means high. It is used in geography to designate part of a village or region higher than the other one . . ."

What adds to the mystery is that I know for a fact that French vintners do ship to the United States wines labeled "haut sauternes." I have seen the bottles.

Be that as it may, the French pronunciation of *"haut"* is, of course, "oh," as in O'Leary or O'Reilly. Most Americans, however, including the vintners who make "haut sauterne," pronounce it "hot."

This might account for an experience reported to me by my late Sausalito neighbor, author Eugene Burns.

Burns and his wife were flying home from the Orient on a Japanese airliner. It was Christmas Eve. When time came for dinner on the plane, the kimono-clad stewardesses brought out a surprise for the passengers. It was a complete holiday dinner, including turkey and

127

all the trimmings. With it they served glasses of sau-terne—piping "haut"!

Right here is as good a time as any to explain still another puzzling term you find on some American sauterne labels: "chateau."

This one began about a century ago, when the only way California vintners could sell their wines in eastern markets was to put counterfeit French labels on them. One such widely imitated label was that of the most famous of all French sauternes, the Château d'Yquem.

As the years passed, California wines gradually achieved recognition for quality in their own right, and the California wine acquired a somewhat more infor-mative label as *"California* Chateau Yquem."

But following the repeal of Prohibition the United States government summarily outlawed the use of all foreign proprietary names on American wines, and "Yquem" was the principal casualty.

What did the California vintners do? Deprived of "Yquem," they preserved "chateau." So now, when you see "chateau" on a California wine label, immedi-ately preceding the name of the vineyard, it does not refer to anybody's feudal castle. All it means is that the wine in the bottle is an extra-sweet California sauterne.

This semantical nightmare about sweetness was cli-maxed with a paradox during the 1940s, when the so-called "kosher" Concord grape wines appeared on the national scene. For these products are made syrupy sweet by massive additions of sugar. Here our govern-ment was faced with a problem, because the quantity of sugar the "kosher" producers used was more than the federal regulations allowed any wine to contain, unless it was called "imitation."

The government decided to permit their sale, but in order to warn the public, decreed that each label must contain the following phrase in capital letters: SWEETENED WITH EXCESS SUGAR.

But to the amazement of all concerned, the public, instead of being warned not to buy, welcomed the promise of extra-sweet wines, and bought them freely—apparently not caring whether the sugar came from grapes, cane, beets, or corn, as long as it was there. In fact, the EXCESS SUGAR phrase helped to make the kosher producers millionaires almost overnight. As they used to say about a certain controversial pianist who was derided by experts for hamming the classics, these winemakers cried all the way to the bank.

Finally the government gave up and dispensed with the "excess sugar" requirement; and the labels now merely read: "specially sweetened."

The kosher-type wines are not the only ones containing added sugar. Most of the flavored "pop" wines and all fruit wines—such as the blackberry, loganberry, and apple types—are similarly sweetened. Also, the grapes grown in eastern and midwestern states and Canada do not develop sufficient natural grape sugar to ferment into standard wines, and consequently they require a moderate supplement of nongrape sugar.

California, however, has long had a vintner-sponsored state regulation prohibiting the addition of sugar to its traditional wine types—and some of the

129

state's vintners are not entirely happy about it, because they have discovered that when wines do need sweetening for any reason, sugar gives them better flavor than grape juice or grape syrup does.

Some of the European countries, too, prohibit adding sugar to wine, or require that the labels show that the wines are sugared. But while it is well known that many European wines (especially French burgundies and German rhine wines) are thus sweetened, I have yet to see a single label that admits it.

This raises the question of what is meant by the legend that appears on millions of wine bottles, proclaiming their contents are "100 per cent pure." Since sugared wines are as eligible as any to claim purity, the phrase seems quite meaningless, and I have heard some vintners express the wish that they had never begun using it. It assuredly does *not* mean that the wines without the "pure" label are in any respect impure.

WHAT ALCOHOLIC CONTENTS MEAN

Historically, some of the earliest pure-food laws were aimed at stopping the adulteration of wines, because synthetic versions of the product have been sold in many countries during periods of grape scarcity. The cardinal, most ancient sin—that of watering wines to stretch their volume—has been stopped, however, at least in the United States, by the federal regulation that requires every bottle to tell you its approximate alcoholic content. When government inspectors find a wine of different alcoholic strength from what the label states, they have a made-to-order case against the offending bottler.

In table wines (sometimes called "light" and "dinner" wines) the alcohol is created entirely by the natural fermentation of sugars and rarely exceeds 14 percent of the wine's volume. The dessert wines, on the other hand, contain brandy (pure wine spirits, distilled from wine), which is added to arrest fermentation before the sugars have completely fermented—thus keeping these wines sweet. Most dessert-wine labels give the alcoholic content as 17, 18, 19, or 20 percent.

However, these figures do not give the exact strength. Because grapes, yeasts, and wines are temperamental, government regulations permit table wines to vary over a range of three percentage degrees, so that "alcohol 12 percent by volume" on a label can mean that the contents of the bottle may actually test as low as 10½ percent or as high as 13½ percent. A leeway of two degrees is permitted on dessert wines, so that "18 percent" really means 17 to 19 percent.

You never see labels with figures above 21 percent, for a very good reason: When a wine exceeds that level, the federal tax suddenly is more than tripled.

In fact, this matter of tax rates helps to explain why the wine "class" names are so confusing—why, for example, the extremely sweet kosher type is nevertheless called a "table" wine, and why dry sherry—although primarily an appetizer wine—is nevertheless lumped with the sweet "dessert" wines.

131

The reason is that the federal government taxes the standard nonsparkling wine types at two different rates, depending on their alcoholic content. (The rates in 1974 were 17 cents per gallon on wines not exceeding 14 percent, and 67 cents per gallon on those between 14 percent and 21 percent.) Since there are thus two distinct tax classes, each class had to have a name. For many years the government called the first group "light wine" and the stronger group "fortified wine." But vintners detested the word "fortified," which gave the public the unfortunate impression that the stronger wines were being purposely spiked to make them more intoxicating. Finally the government was persuaded to rename the groups for the principal uses to which most of the wines are put. Hence, "table wine" and "dessert wine."

But, people keep asking, why do the alcholic content figures on the bottles vary so? Why do some port and sherry labels say 18 percent, others 20 percent, and still others (in a few parts of the nation) read only 16 percent?

Let me first explain the conundrum of the 16 percent port and sherry. Certain states impose local restrictions or special taxes on full-strength dessert wines. Their peculiar laws led, following the repeal of Prohibition, to the creation of low-alcohol wines resembling port, sherry, and other standard dessert wines. The government allowed these confusing variations to be labeled "light port" and "light sherry." Most vintners wish that these strange labels had never come into existence.

All standard sherries and ports must conform to the

132

federal standards, which set 17 percent as the minimum strength for sherries and 18 percent for port and most other dessert wines.

Table wines' alcoholic contents vary most, depending on the sugar content of their grapes. Grapes as sweet as 28 degrees Brix (the scale by which winemakers measure sugar content) can ferment—when completely dry—to about 15 percent alcohol. Grapes of 18 Brix can produce about 9 percent. California, where fully mature grapes are the rule, enforces a minimum of 10 percent alcohol for its white table wines and 10½ percent for its reds; but the federal government allows wines as low as 7 percent. Thus, while most table wines you find in stores are well above the California minimums, you often find wines from Germany, where the grapes are seldom very sweet, and sometimes from France, labeled as containing 9 percent or even less alcohol.

You can expect some of the California minimums to be reduced in years to come. Especially that state's vintners are beginning to notice that those 9 percent German white wines not only have excellent keeping quality, but that some of their delicate flavor stems from their low alcoholic content. The trend is already evident in the flavored "pop" wines, which are exempt from the California minimums; some of them are as light as 8 percent. If the federal 7 percent minimum is ever lowered, as has been proposed, we someday will see 5 percent wines on the market.

The federal regulation allows labels of table wines to omit alcoholic content statements and merely to say "table wine" or "light wine." Most California table wine labels still contain alcohol statements, however, to show that they conform to the state minimums.

How do wines compare in strength with other alcoholic beverages? Beer, of course, is the lowest, ranging usually from 4 percent to 5 percent by volume. Ales and "malt liquors" are usually stronger, ranging from 4.7 to as high as 7.55 percent. Hard cider, the home-made kind, reaches about 7 percent.

Sake, the Japanese rice brew (a beverage that is traditionally served hot), is usually around 16 percent, and is classed by the United States Government as "wine" for labeling purposes and as "beer" for tax purposes.

Vermouths are flavored wines, and vary from 16 percent to 20 percent.

But all of the stronger beverages measure their alcohol in "proof spirits," a term which in the United States is simply double the actual percent of alcoholic content by volume of the drink. So divide each of the following "proof" figures in half to calculate the alcohol by volume: Cordials or liqueurs, 52 to 110 proof. Gins, 80 to 94 proof. Rums, 80 to 151 proof. Vodkas, whiskies, and brandies, 80 to 100 proof. A "bottled in bond" whisky or brandy is always at least 100 proof; that is, 50 percent alcohol.

WHY WINE NAMES ARE CONFUSING

Nothing on a wine label can possibly confuse the public as completely as the names of the wines themselves do. It is easier to explain how the tangle came about than it is to untwist it. The reason is that all winemaking in North and South America (Australia and South Africa, too) began as an art imported from Europe.

With the art came the language of wine. And the language of wine types in Europe—as in the ancient Near East, where wine was born—is mainly a language of geography, not of flavor. In other words, most kinds of wine produced in Europe are named for the places where they are grown.

Thus, burgundy and champagne originated in the French regions so named; port was named by the British for the City of Oporto in Portugal, and sherry is a word the British coined because they could not pronounce the name of the Spanish town from which the wine came—Jerez de la Frontera (originally spelled Xérès).

These names, and many others of origins mainly geographic, spread throughout the civilized world long ago on the labels of the wines. The words became part of other languages. France and Germany adopted port and sherry. Spanish vintners began making *borgoña* and *champaña,* and the European winemakers who emigrated to the New World faithfully named their new wines for their former homelands.

Eventually, the European vintners realized that their treasured wine names were no longer exclusively their own. Alarmed, they demanded that the use of all geographic wine names be restricted to wines produced in the localities the words originally represented. Their

135

governments obliged by entering into international treaties on wine nomenclature. Spain, Portugal, France, Germany, and other nations signed such agreements. Great Britain also obliged, despite loud protests from the young wine industries of Australia and South Africa.

But Europe had awakened too late to win back its names from America. European wine-type names had become permanent parts of the American language over a century ago—along with Russian rye bread, Swiss cheese, Danish pastry, and Dutch ovens.

For decades, and to this day, the French government, in particular, has demanded of the United States State Department, with little effect, that only French bubbly wine should be permitted to be called champagne. French vintners bitterly complain that America not only has pirated French names, but even awards medals to vintners for using them!

The American wine industry's reply is that no imitation is intended—that every label clearly shows that the wine is American, not European—and that vintners here would prefer to use other names, if any existed in their language. Shall we stop calling our dishes china? they ask. Or order our sports writers to cease reporting that the prize fighter's punch drew claret?

To placate the French, the United States government requires American labels to use large type in printing the American place of origin on labels, in direct conjunction with any wine-type name of foreign origin. Labels say "California Burgundy," "American Sherry,"

136

"Ohio Port," "New York State Champagne," et cetera. Further, only a few of these wine-type names are allowed, and all foreign proprietary names (such as Château d'Yquem) are forbidden.

According to my friends in Paris, the French are now hopeful of depriving Canadian sparkling-wine producers of the right to call their product champagne. But thus far France has made no progress whatever in protesting the "Sovietsky champanskoe" produced in Russia.

WHAT GRAPE NAMES MEAN

At this juncture the American wine snob enters the controversy. He displays his erudition by condemning United States wines as "imitations," simply because of the international type names they bear.

Weary of defending themselves, many winemakers, primarily those producing higher-priced wines, have turned to a different kind of label. They now name each wine for the grape variety from which it is made. So now we have such names as White Pinot, Pinot Blanc, Red Pinot, Pinot Noir, and Chardonnay to perplex the public; also Sauvignon Blanc, Green Hungarian, Chenin Blanc, French Colombard, Gamay, Grignolino, Sémillon, Traminer, Elvira, Niagara, Charbono, Sylvaner—to name just a few of these delicious impedimenta to public understanding of wine.

If you cannot spell or pronounce these names, and cannot tell varietally labeled wines apart by tasting them, do not let it trouble you. I assure you that very few people who are not professional experts (and not many of the latter) can actually distinguish, by tasting a white wine, whether it is made of Sémillon, Sylvaner, White Riesling, or Chardonnay grapes. And the average official wine judge will admit his inability, if you administer truth serum (or enough of his favorite wine), to tell Cabernet Sauvignon from Gamay or from Pinot Noir. On the occasions when I happen to identify all of these wines in blind tastings, I swell with pride and brag to my family about my achievement.

In recent years, European vintners have discovered to their alarm that Americans are buying the American "varietals" in preference to comparable French, German, and Italian wines, often paying higher prices for the American products.

This has brought an ironic twist to the nomenclature wrangle. European vintners are now imitating the American labels, renaming their wines, too, for grape varieties and exporting them to the United States. It is the Old World's ultimate recognition of this country's vinicultural success.

Dame Nature being true to her capricious self, there are far too many grape varieties, and variations within varieties, with only faint differences in wine flavor.

At the same time, there are wines of grape varieties that have similar names but that are not of equal quality. For example, there are three grapes called Cabernet: Cabernet Sauvignon, Cabernet Franc, and Ruby Cabernet. The United States government has found it necessary to restrict the use of "Cabernet" on labels to wines of Cabernet Sauvignon. Wines of Ruby Cabernet henceforth must be labeled with the full name of that grape.

There is only one true White ("Johannisberg") Riesling, but wines of three other grapes are allowed to use the "Riesling" name: Franken Riesling (Sylvaner) may be sold as simply "Riesling"; Emerald Riesling, like Ruby Cabernet, must be labeled with its full name. The third is Grey Riesling, whose French name is Chauché Gris.

Meanwhile, in the University of California's vineyard at Davis, Professor Harold P. Olmo has spent four decades marrying old grape varieties to create new ones. He has introduced many, including the just-mentioned Ruby Cabernet and Emerald Riesling, and is testing dozens more that show equal promise.

Grape breeders in France have been doing this for generations. Many of their varieties, hybrids (crosses) of Old World types with American wild vines, have been introduced to our eastern and midwestern states. These French-American hybrids are being made into wines which bear their varietal names. You will find the principal ones identified in the "Key to 362 Wines."

Mistaken identification of grapes contributes to the maze. Many growers (in Europe as well as in America) do not know the right names of their vines. And it is an open secret that when Agoston Haraszthy, the Hungarian "count" who is called the father of modern California viticulture, imported 100,000 cuttings of European vines to his adopted state in 1862, the labels on many of the 300-odd varieties became hopelessly mixed. Not long ago a vintner who had won many customers for his excellent Traminer wine was horrified to learn from university experts that the grapes in his vineyard were not Traminer at all, but a less-known variety called Red Veltliner.

SHOULD THE 51% MINIMUM BE RAISED?

Besides, you may as well know that the average "varietal" wine is not made entirely of the grape whose name it bears. Because wines need blending to achieve flavor balance, the federal regulations permit blending with as much as 49 percent of other varieties. And although the government says the flavor of the variety on the label must predominate, you often find a "varietal" in which the 49 percent overpowers the 51 percent.

The few buyers who know this are indignant and some are rejecting any wine with a grape name unless the label states it is made "entirely" of that grape. Also unhappy are the farmers who grow the costly, light-bearing grape varieties. They want the 51 percent minimum raised to make the wineries buy more of their grapes. Why not raise it to 100 percent? you may ask. That would be a mistake, because fine wines need to be blended with additional grape varieties for balance and complexity. Virtually all fine European wines are blends of different grapes; the best Médoc clarets contain Cabernet Franc and Merlot as well as Cabernet Sauvignon; French champagnes traditionally are blends of Pinot Noir, Pinot Blanc, and Chardonnay; many fine German White Rieslings also contain some

Müller-Thurgau grapes. Everyone now seems agreed that the 51 percent minimum is too lenient, but wineries are disagreed on whether it should be raised to 65 percent or to 75 percent.

Adding to the confusion is the fact that nearly every grape variety has two or more different names. Sauvignon Blanc, for example, is also called Fumé Blanc and Blanc Fumé. Some wineries have been known to make three different wines of the Chenin Blanc grape, naming the other two by its other names, "White Pinot" and "Pineau de la Loire."

The prize case that befuddles everyone is that of the Gamays. Gamay Noir is a grape variety that makes a red California wine that is usually labeled Napa Gamay. Gamay Noir is also the same grape variety from which the famous red wines of the Beaujolais region of France are made. There is also a different grape in California named Gamay Beaujolais, which has nothing to do with Beaujolais wine, but is really one of the many clones of the Pinot Noir. To complete the puzzle, the wine of the Gamay Beaujolais grape is unlike that of either Pinot Noir or Gamay Noir. If you are perplexed about this, you are not alone. Most wine merchants and even most grape growers do not understand it yet.

However, not all grape variety names for wines are necessarily confusing. A few of them have conveyed unmistakable color and flavor meanings for generations. Muscatel, for example, is recognized by almost everyone who has ever tasted it, as a golden 18-to-20-

percent sweet dessert wine with the powerful flavor of Muscat grapes. Wines labeled "Muscat," however, are usually less than 14 percent in alcoholic content, and are somewhat less sweet than Muscatel.

Another "varietal" wine that when well made is readily identified by its aroma is Gewürztraminer, a spicy (Gewürz is German for "spicy") sub-variety of Traminer.

Zinfandel, a grape of mysterious origin (now said to be the Primativo di Gioia of southeastern Italy), gives its name to a popular California claret, in which —if your nose is remarkably sensitive—you sometimes can detect a faintly raspberrylike flavor.

Longfellow sang the praises of Catawba, a white wine (there also are pink and sparkling versions) made from that Labrusca grape, principally in Ohio and New York State.

Vintners who make their rosé wines of Grenache, Gamay, or Cabernet grapes often add those varietal names to their rosé labels.

And when you mention "grape flavor" to most Americans, they automatically think of a single grape—the Concord variety—which provides the taste of the kosher-wine type and of most fresh and frozen grape juices.

Lest my frank explanations be taken to imply that I do not approve of the "varietals," let me add that I generally prefer them. One reason is that many vintners nowadays use varietal labels for the very choicest of their table wines. Another is that, being an

142

oenophile, I find special enjoyment in detecting each grape's personality in a wine. And besides, I like to serve my family and guests as many different wines as possible.

WHAT GEOGRAPHY REALLY MEANS

Returning to Europe's geographic labeling, while place names do not mean everything, as the Europeans claim they do, they do mean something. The climate of Bordeaux is kind to the grape varieties that make red and white Bordeaux wines, and each delimited district within the Bordeaux area has found, by centuries of experience, which grapes thrive best within its borders—the Cabernet Sauvignon, Cabernet Franc, Malbec, and Merlot. Burgundy, on the other hand, best nurtures the Pinots, Gamays, and Aligoté; the Rhone Valley favors the Petite Sirah; Germany's Rhineland makes its best wines from White Riesling. As a result, the European geographic names have—to some extent—a varietal significance.

The flavorful grapes grown in the famed French districts produce only poor wines when planted in southern France, a major source of French *vin ordinaire*. There, consequently, undistinguished, heavy-bearing varieties are mainly cultivated, and the southern French wines are so neutral that vast quantities of wine are imported in tank ships from Tunisia, Algeria, and Morocco for blending. The wine the average French city dweller drinks is a blend of poor French

143

wine and better wine from several other countries.

It is mainly climate that governs a district's ability to grow the superior grapes successfully. The Europeans believe that soil composition is equally important, but modern research questions whether any chemicals in the earth actually enter the flavor of a wine. Yet some soils, such as the gravelly kinds, do hold the sun's heat better than others do, and help grapes to mature.

It might interest the French to know that California, too, is jealous of its name, and that the same applies to individual California localities.

For example, when a California vintner ships 16 percent "light sherry" to a state which discriminates against genuine sherry, he must have special permission from the California Department of Public Health. And in so doing he loses the right to label such wine with the name of California; it may only be called "American" light sherry. And while a "New York State" or "Ohio" wine may contain as much as 25 percent of wine made elsewhere (and many of them are blends with wine or grape syrup from California), no wine can claim to be Californian unless it is made 100 percent in California from California grapes.

Equally jealous of their names are the leading California table-wine districts. The Livermore Valley is noted for its outstanding sauterne types, and its vintners show their district's name on their labels. Napa Valley's name on a label automatically commands higher prices for its table wines, red and white. Sonoma, Santa Clara, Santa Cruz, Mendocino, and Monterey counties are all known to connoisseurs for their distinctive table wines. The Cucamonga district in southern California and the Lodi district in the Central Valley have borrowed a leaf from the French practice, and have persuaded the United States government to recognize specific geographical limits of their viticultural areas for labeling purposes.

The University of California has measured the average annual hours of sunshine in each of the state's vineyard areas, and recommends specific grape varieties that grow best in each locality. This has furnished the scientific explanation of why the state's warm valleys produce the best dessert wines, but why most experts look for their finest table wines in the cooler coastal counties.

Elsewhere in the Americas, districts' climates also determine where grapes are grown and how they taste. In the United States, New York's Finger Lakes district is noted for champagne and other distinctively flavored wines, and the Sandusky–Lake Erie Islands and Cincinnati districts of Ohio have won fame for their special types. Other well-established winegrowing districts are the Yakima Valley and Columbia Basin of Washington, the Willamette and Umpqua Valleys of Oregon, the Missouri River vineyards of Missouri, much of southwestern Michigan, northwestern and southeastern Pennsylvania, portions of New Jersey, Arkansas, Virginia, and the Carolinas. In all, wine is now grown commercially in thirty-one states, and each sells its wine with the claim that its location accounts for distinctive

145

qualities. The successful introduction of the French hybrids by Philip Wagner of Baltimore and of Vinifera vines in the East by Dr. Konstantin Frank of Hammondsport, New York, gives promise that winegrowing soon will spread to several additional areas that apparently have climatic advantages.

The embattled French thus have some support for their argument that place names deserve protection. However, they should have started much earlier. So should the City of Boston, whose chefs are quoted as objecting in vain to the designation of beans, prepared by inexpert cooks in other parts of the nation, as "Boston baked beans."

There are additional sides to this subject of district nomenclature. The ancient wine-laden oxcart is still seen in some of Europe's wine lands, but motor tank trucks are more often seen on the same roads. In both Europe and America we see the growth of large wineries which bring wines from different grape districts to their central cellars for blending and sale under the brands they advertise. Does the spread of swift modern transportation mean that the era of geographic wine labeling is approaching an end?

Obviously France does not think so. The French since 1935 have designated several hundred of their viticultural districts as appellation-controlled, plus some dozens of "V.D.Q.S." districts (*Vins delimités de qualité supérieur*), and are adding more every year. Italy, Spain, and Portugal, seeing that the French controlled-appellation wines bring higher prices than other wines, have adopted the same idea. Wines from

146

controlled Italian regions bear such designations as "D.O.C." (*denominazione di origine controllata*), and Spain is steadily adding new districts with *denominaciónes de origen.*

"*Appellation contrôlée*" and "V.D.Q.S." on French labels are supposed to mean that the contents of the bottle were grown in the delimited district whose name it bears, from approved grape varieties only, and according to the locally recognized method of vinification. Yet there is no one country that imports more wine in bulk for blending with its own production than France does, and the French are known to be better at writing strict laws than at enforcing them.

Apparently, long-suffering Europe has ceased complaining about our tendency to anglicize its wine types. At any rate, the Bordeaux producers have not expressed themselves recently about American vintners' omission of the final "s" in the name of sauternes. But some United States producers take the matter seriously, and their labels always contain the ninth letter, which makes people wonder whether the bottle's contents are plural. Perhaps the Old World feels as Mark Twain did when he said he had no respect for anyone who knows only one way to spell a given word.

But the winegrowers who produce only fine dry white wines around the world-famous village of Chablis in northern Burgundy should be up in arms against the United States Treasury Department office that grants approval of wine labels. When in 1965 the Gallo winery in California proposed to sell one of its two rosés as "pink chablis," that government office promptly granted its approval of the label. Then, as though allowing a world-renowned white wine name to be used on a pink wine was not enough, the same office soon thereafter granted the Italian Swiss Colony permission to label one of its red wines as "ruby chablis."

Aside from thus stretching the meaning of "chablis," American vintners' use of Old World names sometimes makes better sense from the average wine shopper's standpoint than the European labels do.

For example, United States wineries have grown weary of labeling red sparkling wine "sparkling burgundy" while the white and pink sparkling types are champagne and pink champagne. Now, by obtaining a simple change in federal regulations, they have made "sparkling burgundy" synonymous with a new term: red champagne.

Another case is American ports, all of which are at least sweet. The Portuguese have given up trying to persuade other countries to stop calling sweet dessert wines "port," and Portugal now calls its own port wines "porto." But the Portuguese confuse the porto name by also selling a "dry" porto and a "Muscatel" porto.

Another strange instance of involved wine semantics is American tokay, which without any relation to the table grape of that name, came to designate a medium-sweet tawny-pink dessert wine that has no relation, either, to Hungarian tokay. But at least the American name has clearer meaning than the Hungarian (spelled Tokaj or Tokaji), which can signify wines white or red, dry or sweet, or in between.

The job of simplification is far from finished, however. To confuse the average vintner, ask him to tell you the flavor difference among America's rhine wine, chablis, and dry sauterne—or between claret and burgundy. In many cases there isn't any.

THE NEW WINE NAMES

As though the thousands of old wine-type names were not enough, a flood of entirely new ones has hit the national market during the past two decades.

Some are from old-line wineries who have given certain of their distinctive products proprietary names, which they alone can use. Examples are Beaulieu Vineyard's Beaumont for its Pinot Noir and Beauclair for its White Riesling, The Christian Brothers' Château La Salle for its semi-dry muscat table wine, Gallo's Paisano for its popular red vino type, Paul Masson's Baroque for one of its burgundies and Rubion for its light-bodied claret, and Taylor's Lake Country Red, White, and Pink. The trend toward proprietary names, which have the advantage of simultaneously representing both the wine and the brand, is expected to grow in years to come.

Far more numerous are the names of the entirely new wine types with added nongrape flavors designed to please the iced-Cola-and-apple-pie tastes of modern Americans. Most of these products are identified by words in small type like "apéritif wine" and "wine with natural pure flavors." But the coined names they bear, referring to almost anything but grapes, are unlike anything ever before seen on wine labels anywhere.

149

If their success is any indication of the future, these new products may well remodel all old concepts of what constitutes wine.

OTHER LABEL MYSTERIES EXPLAINED

One kind of legend on wine labels that especially puzzles shoppers is the assortment of words supposedly describing variations within a single wine type. The varying sweetnesses of sherries and champagnes, already explained, are one example. Another is the sub-types of port.

White port is easily distinguished from the red, of course. But then we have "tawny" and "ruby" ports as well as the traditional type with no qualifying term. Most tawny ports are what the word implies: tawny in color, presumably from long aging in the cask; but they also sometimes are slightly less sweet than the other sub-types. Ruby port is sometimes sweeter than the others, and is as rich and colorful as its name implies.

The Germans offer an interesting series of qualifying terms for their wines. A wine labeled *Auslese* supposedly means that the grapes were fully ripe and carefully selected and indicates that the wine is semisweet. *Beerenauslese* is a claim that each individual grape berry was carefully selected as perfectly ripe. *Spätlese* signifies that the grapes were left on the vine to become partly raisined and to grow the "noble mold" of French sauternes (Edelfäule in German). *Trockenbeerenauslese* means the same as the other three terms, except that the grapes are almost completely raisined, and the wine is correspondingly very sweet; and while all four mean the wines are expensive, the latter is enormously so.

Another German term has charmed many American buyers because of its literal translation. It is *Liebfrau-milch,* which means "milk of the Blessed Virgin." All it actually tells you, however, is that it is just another German rhine wine, and not necessarily from the most distinguished vineyards. Some of them do not deign to use the word.

Most confusing among European label designations are the "first," "second," "third," "fourth," and "fifth" *crus* (growths) on the labels of leading Bordeaux vineyards. They represent a classification of the region's most famous estates, ranking each in the order of the quality of its wines. The classification was made in 1855. Although many of the chateaux have changed hands and replanted their vineyards during a century, reviews of these rankings since have produced only one change. It was the promotion of Château Mouton Rothschild in 1973 from second to first *cru.* As any book about Bordeaux wines will tell you, many a third or fourth *cru* is conceded to be superior to many a first and second *cru.*

Producers of California's rosés are providing some puzzles, too. Some vintners offer two versions of this pink wine—one called "vin rosé" and the other simply "rosé." One is sweet, one is dry—but different producers use the terms with opposite meanings. Besides, the puzzling word *vin* is merely French for "wine."

"Solera" on some of the sherry labels arouses some curiosity, which is usually answered by explanations

151

on the bottles' back labels. It refers to the Spanish method of fractional blending—an intricate system of aging wines gradually in batteries of small casks, periodically blending portions of new wine with old.

A number of rather ordinary sounding words have special meanings on bottles of wine, and vintners have been known to battle at lengthy public hearings over the right to use them. The public may not notice, for example, that some labels say the wine was "produced and bottled by" a given person, vineyard, or company, while other wineries say "made" instead of "produced," and still other wines simply read: "bottled by . . ."

The significance of "produced" is that the vintner named must have crushed, fermented, matured, and bottled at least 75 percent of the wine in the bottle. Large wineries, however, often exchange wines with one another to maintain balanced inventories and regularly contract with other cellars to produce wines for them, and also buy some wines from bulk producers. So, rather than attempt to segregate for separate labeling the lots fermented in their own cellars, they usually compromise by having all their labels say "made" instead of "produced."

"Bottled at the winery" is another legend of restricted use, meaning much the same as "produced." But "estate bottled" was once the rare designation permitted only for use by the small wine-growing estates. It was equivalent to the French *mise en bouteille au château*, meaning that 100 percent of the grapes were grown in the owner's vineyard and that every drop of the wine was made and bottled in his adjoining cellar. Some wineries still adhere strictly to this meaning and consequently don't have many "estate bottled" wines. But recent federal rulings in individual cases have allowed certain vintners to label whole assortments of wines as "estate bottled" when the grapes came from vineyards they do not own, some of them located many miles away from their cellars. The rulings only limit "estate bottled" to the meaning that the vineyards are in the same county as the winery and that the grapes are grown under the winery's control. But neither is *mise en bouteille au château* any longer a complete assurance of genuine château-bottling in France. Trucks with portable bottling equipment now call each year at some small French wineries, making their bulk wines eligible to be labeled as château-bottled.

In recent years a movement has begun, aiming to persuade the government to tighten the meaning of "estate bottled" to what it originally signified.

Don't let French phrases like *mise en bouteille* on labels give you the impression that they mean "estate bottled" unless they also say *au château* or *au domaine*. Some French wine merchants, knowing that not all Americans have mastered the Gallic language, proclaim on their labels *mise en bouteilles dans nos caves*. All this means is that they bottled the wine in their cellars, that they didn't do it out-of-doors.

Other label mysteries are simple, however, compared to the problem of identifying the producer of a wine when the bottle bears a fictitious trade name. Some of the best wineries play this game of hiding their

153

identities. One well-known vintner during 1974 was bottling his wines under almost a hundred different names—his own and more than ninety others. The bottles bearing his fictitious names were generally priced lower than those identified as his own. Because I happen to recognize them, I usually buy the bottles bearing his aliases. In his case they are real bargains.

Although at first glance this naming practice may seem naughty, there are some good reasons for its existence. Certain store chains regularly contract with wineries and food packers to supply them with merchandise under the chains' private brands. A winery which supplies such a chain may prefer not to be identified. The fictitious trade name is the solution.

There is also the vintner's problem of disposing of that part of his production which is not quite up to his top-quality standard. By selling his second-grade wine under a different name, he avoids injuring his reputation for high quality. This practice, by encouraging the bottling of wine at the winery where it is produced, is better from the consumer's standpoint than the alternative of letting it be shipped somewhere else for bottling.

If you insist on identifying the bottler of a wine that bears a winery name you never heard of, there is one way to get the information. Ask the nearest office of the United States Internal Revenue Service's Bureau of Alcohol, Tobacco, and Firearms. It may take a while to get an answer, however, because while there are in the United States almost five hundred bonded wine cellars besides many wine-bottling houses, there prob-

ably are at least three times as many additional fictitious trade names on bottles of American wines.

TRUTH ABOUT MEDALS

Another thing you often find on labels is the story
of how many medals the wine has won in assorted
fairs and international expositions. This subject is good
for an argument any time you can get two wine men
together. Having been a wine judge at official California competitions—sniffing scores of entries daily, con-
scientiously emptying my mouth to keep a clear palate
for those to follow, and voting for the numbered samples I thought were best—I feel free to join the discussion.

I have no doubt that a wine which has won a gold,
silver, or bronze medal in the annual California judgings was an excellent wine. This is true in spite of a
certain difficulty—the problem of an occasional partly
taste-blind fellow judge. I know one sincere fellow who,
although he served on wine juries for many years,
couldn't tell a Cabernet from a sweet vino. Although
he never realized it, his nerve endings of smell were
insensitive to certain flavors. Fortunately, he is no
longer judging wines.

If you hope to rely on medal awards to guide you
in buying wines you will enjoy, you are likely to be
disappointed, for several reasons.

For one thing, our California juries cannot award
the gold medal to a wine simply because it is the most
delicious wine competing. Instead, judges must search

155

for faults in the wine—including technical faults most consumers could never detect—and finally measure the wine by its conformance to a set of rigid type specifications of color, acidity, astringency, and grape-variety flavor. Often the one wine which would give you the most taste pleasure is thus ineligible for even an honorable mention.

For another, the sample that wins the medal represents a limited quantity of wine in the vintner's cellar; the medal is awarded only on the number of gallons in that lot. So, if you go to the store in your neighborhood to buy a medal-winning wine, your chance of getting the same beverage the judges approved is remote indeed. Connoisseurs who live in California have the best opportunity to buy the prize winners. Some of them go direct to the wineries and snap up whatever medal-winning wine is available.

As for the labels picturing medals awarded to vintages decades ago, they mean only that the winery made fine wine at some time in the past. It probably has good-quality wine now, but this requires proof today.

Moreover, if you merely recall Paris and the golden apple he awarded to Helen of Troy, you remember that any contest depending on human judges' preferences inspires hot controversies, if not open hostilities. So you need not be surprised at the accusations that some vintners enter special lots of wine in the fairs simply to win medals. Nor need you wonder that many of the leading producers refuse to enter all such competitions. Some never have entered. Others have won so many medals in years past that they have simply decided to retire from the lists, like the undefeated ex-champions of sports.

The mature philosophy of Europe offers a contrast to the American fuss over medals. Usually, when wine judgings are held in the Old World, every wine entered gets a medal.

WHAT ARE "MOUNTAIN" WINES?

When you see a label that reads "mountain burgundy" or "mountain chablis," you may wonder whether it really means the wine was mountain-grown.

It once did, but it doesn't anymore. In my book *The Wines of America* I explain this as follows:

In ancient times it was already known that the finest wines are those grown in mountainous regions. Virgil wrote that "Bacchus loves the hillsides." In the United States, Frank Schoonmaker first used "mountain" in 1939 on labels of two wines from the Paul Masson Mountain Vineyard, when he also used "lake" to designate his "varietal" selections from the Widmer Cellars of New York State. Later, "mountain" having never been defined in terms of how high or steep a vineyard should be, the word began to appear on labels of wines made from grapes grown in any of the hilly California coast counties. Then, through the years, "mountain" gradually became the designation of wines sold by coast counties wineries at much lower prices and of lesser quality than their best.

THE STRANGE STORY OF CHAMPAGNE

Omitting several dozen less important kinds of label

157

jargon that other books may eventually explain, I have reserved for the last the remarkable story of sparkling-wine nomenclature.

In France, "champagne" means a white wine of the delimited Champagne district, containing bubbles produced by a secondary fermentation of the wine within the bottle. This involves a lengthy, arduous, and costly procedure, because the secondary fermentation not only produces gas, but also deposits a fine sandlike sediment in the bottle. To get rid of the sediment, the bottles, stored upside down, must be shaken and turned daily for a period of weeks or months until the deposit slides into the bottle's neck. At that point the neck portion is frozen, the cork removed, the sediment disgorged, and the missing wine replaced with more champagne and a *dosage* of sweetening.

In the United States, too, producers must ferment the wine in the bottle if they wish to label it champagne.

But back in 1907 a Frenchman named Eugene Charmat invented a simpler and quicker process which has come into wide use throughout the world. This is the "closed *cuvée*" method, in which the secondary fermentation takes place in large glass-lined tanks, from which the wine is bottled under pressure, conveniently leaving the sediment behind.

But the bulk-fermented wine cannot be labeled champagne as such. The French law calls it only *vin mousseux* (sparkling wine). The United States government's regulation allows it to be labeled *"Sparkling Wine—American* (or local place of origin) *Champagne —Bulk Process,"* and specifies that the extra words be printed on the label in especially prominent letters.

With their more attractive label, you would expect bottle-fermented champagnes to be made of finer wines and to cost more than the bulk-process kind. This is true of some brands, but there are low-priced bottle-fermented champagnes, too. And here is an industry secret.

It is a fact—which all makers of bottle-fermented champagne will hotly deny—that not even the most experienced taster could possibly detect, by eye, nose, or mouth, any difference between a bottle-fermented wine and the *same* wine made bubbly by the simpler process. (I feel compelled to add, thereby incurring the wrath of the users of both the foregoing processes, that the same taster probably would also fail to tell the difference if the bubbles were pumped into the wine by artificial carbonation, as in soda pop.)

The bulk-process vintners constantly clamor to have the annual California wine competitions judge their products together with the bottle-fermented champagnes. The makers of the latter object, and, as of this writing, have still prevented a joint judging.

However, leading producers who use the bottle-fermentation method also age their best champagnes in the bottles before disgorging (removing the sediment caused by fermentation). Prolonged contact with the sediment gives these champagnes a flavor and bouquet different from those not so aged.

Since the 1950s, many producers of bottle-fermented champagnes have adopted the "transfer method," developed in Germany, of removing the sediment without the laborious process of disgorging each bottle. Instead, the bottles are emptied under pressure, the champagne is filtered to remove the sediment, and then is rebottled. Producers who use the old disgorging process label their champagnes "fermented in *this* bottle" and sometimes add still other terms, such as *méthode champenoise.*

This chapter, despite its ambitious title, has "unraveled" only a few of the bewildering terms found on labels of wines. I have attempted in the Glossary at the end of the book to explain several more. But to understand all of the world's leading wine labels, you must be referred to some of the far more complete volumes compiled by some of the other authors whose works are named among my "Suggestions for Further Reading" about the strange world of wines.

12 / You Can Make It Your Hobby

Less strenuous than golf or gardening, better tasting than the backs of old postage stamps, and somewhat more fragrant than my other chief diversion—fishing—is the hobby of wine.

Few other avocations offer as many widely different kinds of pleasure. This one ranges from cultivating your own vineyard to making your own wine; you can tour the world's wine lands; build a wine cellar; collect old labels, fancy stemware; test your palate by tasting—or simply enjoy elbow bending at home.

Wine also blends with gastronomy. All the noted amateur chefs are equally wine hobbyists, because high cuisine demands wine both as a seasoning and as an accompaniment at the table.

As for literature, few kinds of reading offer more pleasure to the senses than recollections of great vintages artfully blended with memorable meals. Wine libraries contain the whole history of civilization.

The wine hobbyist experiences the subtler joys. He

161

sees in his glowing wine the sky over vineyard hillsides; he inhales from it the essence of the countryside; he savors its bouquet, admires it as a work of art, and lets it infuse sunshine into his veins.

It is my hope that this book—which is written to unscramble wine for those Americans still unacquainted with the beverage of civilized, temperate people—will attract more genuine hobbyists to the nectars of the grape. For unlike the overcrowding of my favorite fishing holes, the more devotees of wine, the merrier.

Foremost among the vinous pastimes, of course, is the collecting of fine wines. To this subject I devote most of the later chapter about wine cellars, which also explains such things as storage temperatures, the buying of wines for aging, and when to open an aging wine. But you may not even need your own cellar if your wine merchant happens to have a proper space in which to store wines for you. An increasing number of dealers in our larger cities are equipping their establishments to do so, and are offering this service at a modest monthly charge per case.

The experience of visiting wineries has attracted millions to the fascinating hobby of wine. A hospitable welcome, with tasting, awaits you at most of the world's wineries, not only in America, but in Europe, Australia, and South Africa as well. Travel is most pleasurable when your trip has a theme, and few tours are as delightful as a wine tour can be. Photography and painting blend especially well with wine vaults and vineyards. Vintage scenes, ancient cellars, and the most beautiful of all fruits—the grape—have charmed artists since the beginning of time.

Wine tastings are another delicious way to begin. Join a tasting club, such as Les Amis du Vin (there are many others), or start your own. There are thousands of small groups who gather at one another's homes, sharing the cost of the wines they taste. Holding a home blind-tasting, as suggested in an earlier chapter, is a novel and inexpensive way to entertain.

Gourmet dining also inspires interest in wines. I have many friends who are members of groups devoted to the culinary arts. Some of them hold periodic "everybody-cook" dinners, at which each does his share of the food shopping and preparation. One member, the *sommelier*, is in charge of the wines, and another with artistic talent creates an ornamental menu, which everyone autographs as a treasured souvenir of the feast.

But the most popular of all wine hobbies is making your own wine at home. It is legal and tax-free, so long as you make and possess no more than two hundred gallons and sign a form at the nearest office of the Internal Revenue Service, which not everyone bothers to do. In the past, home winemaking was practiced mainly by immigrant European families to whom wine was a mealtime necessity and who had to make their own during the Prohibition era. Today's avocational winemakers are a different breed. While some are merely saving money, by far the vast majority are people bitten by the wine bug, motivated not by economy but by their fascination with the mystique and romance of wine. The most devoted ones are physi-

163

cians, engineers, chemists, college professors, accountants, and writers, and the doctors are the most avid of all. They find in this scientific kind of handicraft a hobby of continuing interest. Wine gives the winemaker a sense of the future that no other hobby does because the product keeps changing and takes months and years to mature.

How many home winemakers are there? Nobody knows, but I have heard estimates that as many as half a million American householders now make wine more or less regularly in their homes. They even hold homemade-wine competitions, and I have enjoyed serving as a judge at three such events. They are not publicized, because a federal regulation requires the contestants to get permission to participate, since it is illegal otherwise to transport homemade wine from the maker's dwelling. Another provision of the regulation restricts the home-winemaking privilege to heads of households. Bachelors of both sexes have long protested this and are backing a proposed federal law that would remove the discrimination. If these legal obstacles are removed, we can expect national homemade-wine contests to take place in the future, such as those that attract thousands of participants in Britain, where scores of national amateur champions are crowned each year.

This is a hobby that wives should encourage, since it keeps husbands home in the cellar at night. But the product of the expert home vintner can also be very good. I have tasted entries in the competitions that were as fine as commercial premium wines of corresponding types. The product also can be poor, especially when it begins turning to vinegar—in which case one can adopt still another challenging hobby, the making of good wine vinegar at home.

You can ferment almost any kind of fruit or vegetable as well as grapes. Your grandmother and great-grandmother probably used dandelions, rhubarb, elderberries, blueberries, or honey (to make mead). Winemaking is one of the oldest of all the household arts.

Purists, of course, prefer to make their wines of fresh grapes or fresh juice, which can only be bought at vintage time. Grape syrup, called concentrate, is more convenient and is available year round. Everything you need is available from home-winemaking supply stores, of which there probably is one in your neighborhood. Some of the big department stores also now have special sections that display winemaking supplies.

You can start with a beginner's kit, which contains a quart of concentrate, small envelopes of yeast and chemicals, fermentation locks, siphon hose, a collapsible plastic jug, and a recipe to make a single gallon (five bottles) of table wine. If you take this up in earnest, you can buy much bigger kits, and then go on to buy stoneware crocks, jugs, carboys, barrels, bottles, corks, crusher, press, and testing instruments, such as my neighbors own. You can also buy labels printed with your name and such legends as "Château Smith Vin Rouge" or "Maison Jones Private Stock."

Concentrate wines are the easiest to make, and if well made are similar to ordinary commercial types,

165

lacking mainly the aroma of wines made directly from grapes. You can even buy plastic jugs of "varietal" concentrates of the most prestigious grapes, including Cabernet Sauvignon and Chardonnay.

What you especially need is a book of instructions, and I recommend that you buy at least two, because studying both will help you to understand the science as well as the art. Sanitation and meticulous care are the keys to success. Among the highly-regarded books are *Guidelines to Practical Winemaking* by Julius Fessler of Oakland, California, the best for those using California grapes; *American Wines and Wine Making* by Philip M. Wagner of Baltimore, for those who ferment French hybrid and Labrusca varieties; and *The Art of Making Wine* by Stanley F. Anderson of Vancouver, B.C., for those who use grape concentrates. They even tell you how to make your own champagne.

Highly though I recommend this hobby, my vineyard-touring, tasting, and fishing have prevented me from taking up winemaking thus far. My connoisseur daughter is determined, however, that we soon must begin to make our own.

I only bottle wine, buying it from the few wineries that are willing to sell it in bulk. Bottling is also a worthwhile hobby and provides an excuse for holding bottling parties, at which the neighbors participate and take home their share of the wine. I even have my own labels, which read *Koinos Logos,* which is Greek for "Common Sense."

If you decide to try wine bottling, I have three bits of advice: First, let the wine rest; then siphon it off the sediment that should be allowed to settle at the bottom of the demijohn or barrel. Second, make certain your bottles are thoroughly washed, fully sterile, and dry. Third, buy only the best silicone-coated straight corks, which you can insert with an inexpensive hand corker. If the wine is good enough to age and if you bottle it properly, you can enjoy it for years.

The truest of all wine lovers are those who grow their own wines, starting with the grapes. If you have the space at home, plant a vine or two, or a hundred vines if you want enough wine to accompany your dinner throughout the year. You will need patience, however, because it takes three to four years for a vine to produce a crop, and additional time for the new wine to mature. But the rewards are infinitely greater than those from raising other crops that you cannot drink.

Thousands of homeowners in most states of the Union are doing this nowadays. Some of their vines are in corners of back yards, some even in boxes on the terraces of skyscraper penthouses, while others have added vineyards to country estates. Many of these amateur winegrowers are members of the American Wine Society, an organization dedicated to the advancement of their hobby. There is even a magazine published for them, *The Purple Thumb,* at Van Nuys, California. If you want to grow your own wine, first consult your county agricultural agent and your state college horticulture department about which grape varieties are suited to your microclimate and soil, and write the American Wine Society at Royal Oak, Michigan, for its bulletins listing suppliers of vines and everything else you need to become an avocational winegrower.

Which reminds me of the letter a language purist wrote to a newspaper editor, criticizing an article the paper had published about winegrowing. The critic complained that wines are made—that only the grapes are grown. A winegrower read the purist's letter and replied to the challenge, as follows:

> "You don't grow wine," the critic said,
> "What you grow is in the grape."
> "But," we reply, "grapes ARE wine,
> Just in a different shape."

Many other vinous diversions are available without the effort of making wine or growing grapes. A library of wine and food is especially worthwhile. You can keep abreast of vinicultural progress through such journals as *Wines & Vines, Vintage,* and *Wine World,* and with gastronomy in the pages of *Bon Appétit* and *Gourmet.* I have seen marvelous collections of great menus, and have often thought of compiling a volume of historic toasts. (Toasting began, I have read, in ancient Greece, where guests poured a little wine into their hosts' glasses as a precaution against being poisoned. The custom got its name in the sixteenth century, when a bit of toasted bread was dropped into the wine when someone was to be honored.)

The history of wine is replete with odd and interesting facts. Kissing is said to have been invented by Roman husbands checking up on their bibulous wives.

The first French Republic named a month *Vendé-miaire* for the vintage season. The custom of christening a ship by smashing a bottle of champagne on the bow at the launching presumably was a development from the human sacrifices once made to assure the benevolent protection of pagan gods. Red wine came into use as a substitute for blood, but champagne was later substituted because, being more expensive, it was held in higher esteem. Superstitious sailors will tell you of "jinx ships," christened with spring water during Prohibition, which subsequently suffered mishaps or were wrecked.

Creating mixed drinks is a good hobby if you don't swallow everything you mix. One of my doctor friends makes his own apéritif by adding a tablespoon of quinine-based bitters to a bottle of light-bodied port. He also finds that wines blend pleasantly with hard as well as soft drinks, the classic example being the manhattan cocktail, which is whisky or brandy plus sweet vermouth.

The making of May wine provides an occasion for both a picnic and a German or Viennese spring festival. You first go to the woods and search around the trunks of oaks for *Waldmeister* (woodruff), an herb bearing a white jessamine flower with a perfume similar to new-mown hay. Bruise the leaves, add sugar or simple syrup, and any white wine—also orange juice if you like—and after various periods of steeping, you have an exceedingly fragrant drink.

A simpler recipe describes an economical way to make champagne if you happen already to own the

169

piece of equipment required. Put white wine, with a little sugar added, into one of those glass pressure bottles that come with cartridges of carbon-dioxide gas. I have tasted the result, and if the bubbles in the wine were longer lasting (which they could be if the wine were refrigerated overnight), you might not tell it from inexpensive champagne.

Let us return to the subject of home tastings, which I have only touched on thus far.

To set up a tasting, you need glasses (if you haven't enough, you can buy stemmed plastic types), pitchers of water for rinsing glasses between wines, something into which glasses can be emptied, and paper napkins. It is also customary to set out bowls of French bread cut into one-inch cubes, and platters of cheese, preferably mild enough not to clash with the wines.

The number and kinds of wines depend on the group. If the people are new at wines, give them a range of types. If they are knowledgeable about wines, give them several of the same type to compare. If the tasting is a cooperative event, each guest can be asked to bring one of the wines.

People will circle around the tasting table and can pour for themselves. A taste is only an ounce or so, so you don't need a great deal of wine. The total quantity needed will average about a half-bottle per person, so if eight wines are to be tasted, a bottle of each wine should suffice for a party of sixteen.

I recommend making the event a blind-tasting game, masking the bottles as illustrated on page 37. Supply paper and pencils, let the guests try to identify the wines, and at the same time ask them to write down their preferences, marking their first choice as "1."

When everyone has tasted, the bottles are unveiled. A prize can be given to whoever correctly identifies the most wines, and the guests are likely to be surprised at learning which wines they preferred.

An added feature that I have found popular is a test in which each person is blindfolded and asked to distinguish between a white wine and a red by taste. Few people can do this unless they happen to know what flavor to look for, which is told in the chapter on how to taste.

After the tasting, it is customary to serve refreshments, such as canapés and dips. A note of celebration can be added by opening champagne.

13 / How to Glamorize Your Cooking

If you were to visit all the famous chefs in hotels and restaurants throughout the western world, you would find wine in all of their kitchens. Ask any of these masters of cuisine, and they will tell you that wines are indispensable ingredients of their art. All of the best cookbooks published in recent years contain numerous recipes calling for wine.

Yet if you were to visit many average American homes and check the contents of their kitchens, you would find that fewer than half of them use wine in cooking at all. Although the serving of wine with meals has spread nationwide during the past decade, its use has not yet become an integral part of home cooking. The reason is that American homemakers somehow have the impression that to cook with wine requires adherence to especially tested recipes and some special kind of expertise with wines.

The fact is that most uses of wine in cooking require

no recipes whatever, while truly fine cookery is impossible without the use of wine.

Wine is a seasoning like herbs and spices, but in liquid form. Like these other seasonings, wine imparts magic flavors and aromas to foods. But wine is even more, because it accents, brings out and improves natural food flavors, and creates many rich new ones. It also adds a certain flair, even a kind of glamour, to ordinary cooking. Yet it is one of the easiest of all the seasonings to use. Instead of adding water, which is tasteless, to food, you simply replace some of it with wine. The result is a much more fragrant, better-tasting dish.

You need no detailed recipe to prepare the mushroom soup you buy in a can. The directions say to add a can of water. Instead of only water, include a few spoonfuls of sherry. Try it and you will see what I mean.

There is an old saying that "water never added anything but length to a broth." When a broth recipe calls for water, for some of it, substitute wine.

When poaching fish, there is good advice in the old Italian proverb, "Since fish thrive in water, they should be drowned in wine." When I poach fish, I do it in wine or in a wine court bouillon.

When you fry hamburgers, remove the patties and add a quarter-cup of red wine to the skillet. Scrape up the bits of meat, bring the wine to a boil, pour it over the patties, and you have a gourmet dish.

All stews demand wine; roasts basted with it are subtly improved; even baked beans are improved by

173

a little cream sherry, and you can substitute white wine for some of the milk in the sauce for your macaroni and cheese.

As for seafood (the kind of cooking I, as an ardent fisherman, do oftenest), you need only be reminded that most fishes have odor like—well—fish. Add white wine, or better yet, marinate a few hours or overnight in wine, and you discover that the wine breaks down those odorous fishy oils. It is the acid in the wine that does it, just as lemon juice or vinegar does; but the wine also adds its delicate fragrance.

If you insist on testing what I say, try my recipe for baked fish fillets. I use it for striped bass, about which I once wrote a book, but it fits any white-fleshed fish equally well:

Striped Bass Baked in White Wine

In a glass bowl sprinkle 2 pounds of fish fillets with salt and pepper. Cover with slices of a large onion. Add 1 cup dry white wine and let marinate overnight. Melt 3 tablespoons butter in a shallow baking dish. Remove fillets and onion to the baking dish, cover with slices of 2 tomatoes and slices of half a green pepper. Sprinkle with salt. Add 2 tablespoons Worcestershire sauce to the wine in which the fish was marinated. Bake the fish in a preheated 375-degree oven, basting frequently with the marinade containing Worcestershire, until the fillets flake and are no longer translucent (about 35 minutes; don't overcook!) Makes four large or six smaller servings. Serve with dry white wine. Especially tasty when served cold.

Sometimes fowl, too, retains an odor after it has been

cooked. I haven't yet tried marinating chicken before broiling, though I am told it is a good idea. But I make certain of pleasant fragrance when I prepare the following, my favorite chicken dish:

CHICKEN SAUTÉ SEC VIN BLANC

Have a 3-pound frying chicken cut into pieces for serving. Dust with flour seasoned with salt and pepper. Melt 4 tablespoons butter in a heavy skillet. Add chicken and sauté until golden brown, turning the pieces frequently and adding more butter if necessary. Add 2 finely chopped shallots or green onions, 2 tablespoons chopped parsley, and a half cup of dry white wine. Sprinkle with thyme and basil, cover tightly and simmer for 30 minutes. Drain a 4-ounce can of sliced mushrooms. Add the mushrooms and continue cooking for 15 minutes or until the chicken is tender and no liquid remains in the pan. Makes 3 or 4 servings. Serve with the same white wine.

Meats can be tenderized as well as flavored by soaking in red wine. This is an extra reason to marinate pot roasts, meanwhile adding other flavorings, too. Turn the meat occasionally. When you're ready to cook it, strain the marinade and use some of it as part of the liquid in cooking the meat.

My favorite beef dish is burgundy beef, but I like to call it by its French name:

BOEUF BOURGUIGNON

Cut 2 pounds lean beef into 1-inch pieces and shake in a bag with seasoned flour. In a heavy skillet fry 4 bacon strips until tender, cut into pieces and place in a casserole.

175

In the skillet containing bacon fat, brown the beef pieces thoroughly and add to the casserole. Pour 1½ cups dry red wine into the skillet and bring to a simmer, scraping up the bits of meat and flour sticking to the skillet. Pour wine and scrapings into the casserole, adding 3 tablespoons dry vermouth. Then add the following: 2 cloves crushed garlic, 1½ teaspoons salt, 4 bruised peppercorns, 3 cloves, ½ bay leaf, ½ teaspoon each of thyme and marjoram, 12 small onions, 4 new potatoes peeled and cut into serving-size pieces, 4 medium-size carrots cut into 1-inch slices, 2 tablespoons chopped parsley. Cover and cook in a pre-heated 275-degree oven 3 to 4 hours or until beef is tender. Meanwhile in another skillet, brown ½ pound sliced fresh mushrooms in butter, and add them to the casserole 15 minutes before serving. Makes 4 to 6 portions. Serve with dry red wine.

Roasts call for basting, and I find basting them with wine adds zest to their flavor and helps retain their original juices. For roast fowl, I usually baste with sherry or dry white wine, but I baste roasting turkey with red. Some of my friends prepare a basting sauce of butter and white wine or rosé, adding a pinch of herb and perhaps a squeeze of lemon or lime. Kept heated in a small pan, this sauce is brushed over whatever is being cooked.

What kinds of wine are best for cooking? This is a reasonable question, because you can't be expected to keep a whole shelf of different wines in the kitchen, and you remember that table wines will lose quality if kept open very long. The standard wine for most cookery is dry sherry, and with its higher alcoholic content, it keeps well after opening. Another standby is dry vermouth, which is a wine with herbs already added and, like sherry, doesn't spoil when left open. It is suitable for most cooking uses.

You probably have seen special cooking wines for sale in stores, but you don't need them. Cook with the same wine you drink. The difference in the cooking wines is that they have salt added. Some restaurant chefs buy them simply to keep the help from drinking up the kitchen supply.

Many classic recipes call for madeira wine because the recipes have been handed down since colonial days, when madeira was the first wine to become popular in this country. But the best Portuguese madeiras are very expensive, and besides, the recipes don't tell you which madeira—one of the dry types or the sweet—to use. You usually will find that a medium-dry sherry will give you much the same flavor required by the madeira recipes.

How much should you pay for a wine that you intend to use only in cooking? My answer is that I would never add a ten-dollar-a-bottle wine to a dish that I was going to heat, because the extra-delicate bouquet that might have made the wine worth ten dollars would be lost when the heat was applied. But neither will I cook with any wine that is not perfectly delicious to drink. For such a dish as boeuf bourguignon, any sound, inexpensive young red with balanced flavor will do. But if the wines are not to be heated—for example, when added to fresh fruit—I use some of the finest wines I have.

177

Fruit desserts are among the most delicious uses for wine. Sprinkle melon balls with powdered sugar, add port wine to half-cover them, and chill. Or sugar strawberries lightly and add any chilled white wine, cream sherry, or perhaps pink champagne for extra glamour, for a delicious dessert. For my Sunday breakfast I sometimes sprinkle port or cream sherry over my chilled half-grapefruit.

Foods you cook with wine should never smell principally of wine. Don't drown the food, any more than you would add too much of any other seasoning. All you want is the subtle, elusive, usually unidentifiable aroma.

Soups, which I have mentioned only briefly, are among the best uses for sherry. The leading canned soups already contain sherry, part of the manufacturers' secret recipes. Add the sherry to the soup a moment before you serve it. And here is another bit of glamour: just before serving the soup, add another tablespoon of sherry to each empty plate.

People who are worried about calories need not hesitate to cook with wine, because the alcohol, which contains the calories, has a low boiling point and evaporates when heat is applied. This is also the answer to those who, frightened by Prohibitionist propaganda, are afraid to let their children have any alcoholic beverage. A dish cooked with wine has no alcohol left.

14 / How to Build, Enjoy, and Profit from Your Wine Cellar

"**A**ge appears to be best in four things: old wood best to burn, old wine to drink, old friends to trust, old authors to read." So wrote Francis Bacon (1561–1626), attributing this wisdom to Alonso of Aragon.

Old wines are indeed like old friends, since we appreciate them most as they mature with years. Wines and friends, if they have quality when young, become gradually mellow as they mature and reveal facets of character—subtle, complex layers of flavor—that are only hinted at during their youth.

The extent to which fine wines gain smoothness with age can be likened to the difference between wood merely planed and the same wood sandpapered; their gain in bouquet compares to that between rosebud and full-blown flower; their gain in depth of character to that between a youth and a wise adult. Here is the principal delight in the entire sphere of wine.

If you wish to store wines for your future enjoyment,

you need a wine cellar. Wineries age their wines in tanks and casks and some for an extra year or two in glass, but few vintners anywhere can afford to age wines for many years in bottles, where the greatest improvement in drinking quality takes place. If wineries did so, their prices would rise to levels far above what most buyers are willing to pay. You therefore should buy your wines young and age them in a cellar of your own.

But perhaps you are not now planning a cellar and are only interested in keeping a few bottles on hand to save extra trips to the store. Yet you want to keep those bottles in good condition, so you need at least the equivalent of a cellar. By this I mean a place where the wines will not be exposed to light or heat, especially to sunlight, because they thus would become oxidized; and you need a way to keep corked bottles lying on their sides. (Screw-capped bottles should stand up.)

Your mini-cellar need not be more than a chest drawer, or the corner of a cupboard, or a cool spot under the basement stairs. If you prefer to have your bottles in view, there are many kinds of handy wine racks you can buy. You see them on display in numerous beverage, novelty, and department stores. Some come in units that you can assemble to any size you desire.

A closet shelf can be converted to a cellar with a row of fiberboard mailing tubes or of large-size juice cans, which are just the size to hold a bottle each. Drain tiles, obtainable at building supply stores, are also the right size, fit together neatly on a shelf, or can be

Handy 12-bottle rack you can buy in units.

Another type of rack that fits anywhere.

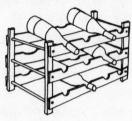

Wire racks are sold in connecting units. Some have gates and locks.

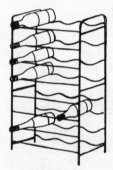

Or just store your wines in chest drawers.

assembled in stacks with some form of support. A cabinet in your living or dining area can be converted to an attractive cellar by cutting a board into pieces to divide the space into bins.

If you have woodworking talent and tools, you can fashion handsome scalloped racks that display single bottles, such as those you see in restaurant wine cellars. But the easiest of all ways to store wines is simply to leave them in the corrugated twelve-bottle cartons, with dividers inside, in which they come from the winery. Simply cut off the flaps so the bottles will be

181

in view. (Keep the bottle necks facing you, and if you see any leaking, open those bottles and drink the wine. Don't store bottles upside down, because this may cause them to leak.)

To store the most wine in the least space, I prefer wooden bins, which I have built in my cellar with 1″ x 12″ boards. It is a good idea to drill a few holes in the boards to provide air circulation. The bins can be either square or in the honeycomb shape that you see in many restaurant wine cellars and beverage stores. The only disadvantage of bins is sometimes having to disturb some bottles if you want to get at one at the bottom of a bin.

Use mailing tubes or juice cans between closet shelves. Agricultural tiles fit together in stacks.

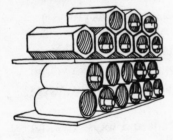

To convert an existing cabinet, cut 1 x 12 planks to divide the space.

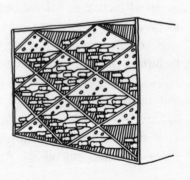

Honeycomb bins, built of 1 x 12 planks, store the most wine in the least space.

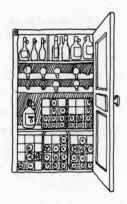

In a closet wine cellar, screw-capped bottles stand upright, and corked wines can be stored in their cartons.

WHAT'S A 'PERFECT' CELLAR?

Seven qualities make a perfect wine cellar: (1) It is reasonably dark; the bottles are not exposed to ultra-violet light. (2) It is cool, ideally around 55° Fahrenheit, but even 70° won't ruin your wines. (3) Whatever the temperature, it should be reasonably constant; it should not rise and fall much with the weather, and especially it should not go down to freezing; the flavors of fine wines have been injured when stored below 40°. (4) The place should be free of vibration because wines improve most and last longest when they lie quiet, undisturbed. (5) It should be ventilated, free from strong odors which the wines might absorb through the corks over a period of time. (6) It should not be excessively moist unless you don't mind the glue loosening and letting the labels fall off your bottles. If mold forms on the corks, however, it won't spoil your wine. (7) The place can be kept locked or is otherwise secure.

183

In other words, if you can just spare a closet that doesn't get too warm and isn't constantly jolted with vibration from passing traffic, you can store a good assortment of aging wines through your lifetime in your apartment or flat.

The warmer your cellar, the faster your wines will age. Conversely, the cooler the cellar, the longer it will take wines to develop their bouquet. The chief advantages of a cool cellar are that your wines will be finer when they mature and that wines already mature may retain their fragile quality for extra years. (If you are paying a wine merchant to store wines for you, it is worthwhile to learn the temperature of his cellar, too.)

In earlier days, houses normally had cellars, and wine cellars were provided in the mansions of the rich. With wine now growing in popularity, some architects are beginning again to provide wine cellars in their plans. Some of the new apartment houses offer wine-cellar lockers for their tenants. Of course, the traditional place to store wines is underground, where temperatures may vary little if at all. This is why we call any place for wine storage a cellar. Today, however, we have insulating materials and air-conditioning equipment, which can achieve the same effect. For example, all modern wineries are now built above ground and many of them even have their tanks outdoors, but such tanks are insulated and some have temperature-controlled water circulating inside their shells.

There also now are air-conditioned wine-cellar cabinets and chests you can buy for your home, equipped with racks and trays to hold hundreds of bottles free of vibration and at 55°. All you do is plug the cord in an electric outlet. The cabinets are attractive pieces of furniture and have sturdy locks. You will find them advertised in wine magazines.

You also can buy the cooling units separate from the cabinets and create a temperature-controlled cellar anywhere you can find the space. A single such unit can cool a sufficiently insulated 600-cubic-foot room. Don't try to keep your cellar cool with the type of air-conditioner that brings in air from outdoors. The best air-conditioning for a wine cellar cools and circulates the cooled air within the cellar. And don't try to adapt an old refrigerator for wine storage because ordinary refrigeration extracts moisture and increases the evaporation of wines through the corks. A cooling unit may not be necessary in an unusually temperate climate where your cellar only warms several degrees during occasional heat spells. In that case you might consider installing an exhaust fan with automatic timing to bring in sufficient cool air during the early-morning hours.

Each wine, like each human being, animal, or plant, has a different life span. It matures at its own rate, reaches its peak of quality, remains there as on a plateau for a time, gaining little except extra mellowness, and eventually begins to grow feeble and gradually to decline. I have developed a graph that illustrates this. The rate at which all this occurs depends on the wine type, the grape variety, where it was grown, and the care the grapes and the wine have received.

As the graph indicates, rosés usually have the shortest lives. White wines are next. The average white, even if ideally stored, is unlikely to retain its freshness or to gain appreciably in quality for much more than a year or two. Only the exceptional whites gain quality with age: the finest Chardonnays, Sauvignon Blancs, and the best French sauternes. Some White Rieslings also improve in the bottle, but few other German wine types are likely to last very long. Chardonnay is unique in that it seems to require a year in the cask and one to three years of bottle age before it reaches a peak and all at once releases its rich bouquet. Yet by age six few Chardonnays are likely to gain further quality,

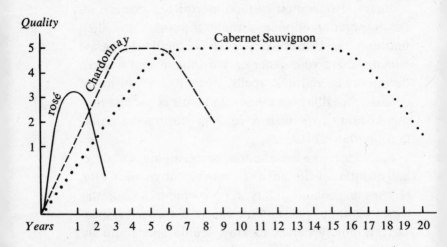

How fine wines age This graph illustrates roughly how the finest red and white wines, such as Cabernet Sauvignon and Chardonnay, improve with age in bottles for years and eventually decline. Most rosés, however, reach their prime early and begin to fade.

and most of them have already started to go downhill.

Champagnes are not expected to improve much after they leave the winery, and in particular should be drunk immediately if they have plastic closures. Yet I have opened top-quality ten-year-old champagnes and found them still in good condition, their color showing their age slightly, but they have had no oxidized taste.

Among the red wines, Beaujolais and Gamay Noir are both intended to be consumed young and are not expected to improve with age. Cabernet Sauvignons and the finest red Bordeaux best exemplify the red wines that can improve for many years. Pinot Noirs and French red burgundies are also intended to be aged, but they do not have the longevity of fine Cabernet Sauvignons. Zinfandels vary; some are best when young and fresh while others have been known to age like the noble Cabernets. Spanish and Italian reds usually come already aged to their maximum as indicated by their vintage dates, but most of their maturing time has been spent in casks. Some Barolos, however, warrant further aging in glass.

Vintners discovered centuries ago that madeiras and sherries transported in sailing ships improved on long voyages. It became customary to load casks of these wines in the holds of ships as ballast and let them travel around the world. The reason for their improvement is apparent when you remember that these are purposely oxidized wines. The best sherries and madeiras are aged for many years in oak casks, but once bottled, they are not supposed to improve. Yet I have some California sherries that have improved greatly since I bottled them decades ago.

But there is no certainty about how wines of different types will age. In fact, you are likely to find differences even between bottles of the same vintage, from the same winery, that come to you in the same shipping case. How can this be explained? One bottle might have a bit more or less air under its cork. Or, when first bottled and not yet packed in a case, it might have been stored higher in a stack while another bottle was exposed to colder air nearer the floor. These differences in headspace or temperature were slight when the wines were young, but they caused major differences in flavor when the wines were aged for many years. "There are no good wines, only good bottles," is a saying among old French winegrowers, quoted by Gerald Asher in *Gourmet*.

WHICH WINES TO BUY FOR AGING

How, then, can you decide which red wines to buy for aging in your cellar? Should you watch the advertisements for sales of cut-price wines? Or let your wine merchant decide for you? Or just settle for Cabernet Sauvignon or Zinfandel because these have the reputation of improving with age?

A cut-price import on sale may have come from a bankrupt stock somewhere and may have been injured by improper handling and storage. But if its name, year, shipper, and importer seem respectable, it is not necessarily to be ruled out. Fluctuations in the wine market are always worth watching if you buy a great deal of wine, because, as pointed out earlier, wine prices go up and down with the size of each year's crop of grapes.

The soundest way to choose a young wine to lay down for aging, unless you let your merchant decide, is to get at least two experts to taste it, or else to taste it yourself. Buy one bottle, take it home, and look carefully for the following elements, which—my professional friends agree—will indicate whether or not a red wine is likely to improve with age:

Does it come from a premium table wine district and from a winery that is unlikely to have stretched it with cheaper hot-region grapes?

Is it lacking in color? Does it show any browning? If it is young, its color should be ruby red.

Has it any off-smells or tastes, especially of vinegar or oxidation? Don't reject it, however, for the strong fermentation bouquet that characterizes many young reds, because this odor eventually will go away.

Has it fragrance? When young, it should have the outstanding character of a grape variety, such as Cabernet Sauvignon.

Has it plenty of fruit acidity, body, and tannin— enough tannin so that you feel the astringent effect in your mouth? It may be rough and undrinkable now, but if it lacks enough tannin, it is unlikely to improve with extended age.

If the wine has passed these tests, run, don't walk, as I advised in an earlier chapter—and buy the rest of the case. Better yet, buy at least two cases, because while a wine is aging you should open a bottle every year or two to observe its progress.

WHEN IS IT READY TO DRINK?

When you have laid the wine down, the next question will be: when will it be ready to drink? This is a guessing game. It depends first on the temperature of your cellar; at 70° the wine will age considerably faster than at 50°. It also depends on the size of the bottle; in a half-bottle, wine ages much faster than in a bottle, and in a bottle much faster than in a magnum (the two-bottle size). This is because the more air to which the surface of a wine is exposed in the bottle, the less time it takes to age.

An aged wine is generally ready to drink when it has developed its bouquet. But when that is likely to occur is only a guess. In earlier days, my Beaulieu Cabernet Sauvignons ripened six to eight years after the vintage, but my Inglenooks did not bloom with bouquet until age eleven. My Bordeaux clarets ripened at ages similar to the California wines, my Saint-Emilions sooner than my Médocs.

Since the Second World War, however, the leading Bordeaux producers have changed their output to lighter, early-maturing wines by increased blending with lighter wines such as Merlot, and also by drawing the wine off the grape skins before fermentation is complete. Some of the California premium producers have now done the same.

As for California Pinot Noirs and Côte d'Or red

burgundies, six years now seems the age by which all of them should bloom, and I have found many of them at their peak by four. The best answer to this question is experience; ask a knowledgeable wine merchant, or someone who owns the same wine of earlier vintages, what his experience has been.

HOW LONG WINES CAN IMPROVE

Finally come the questions connoisseurs discuss endlessly: when a wine has matured in glass and developed its bouquet, can it continue to improve? How much longer will it remain delicious to drink? When will it start downhill?

I have not known red wines in my cellar (60 to 65 degrees F.) to improve beyond twelve to fifteen years of age, and not many of my reds have lasted that long. But many of my friends, veteran wine tasters, say they have wines that have improved for twenty and thirty years, and that they have sampled sixty-year-old reds which had not yet reached their peak of quality. Magnums of Château Lafite, undisturbed in cold cellars, have been known to be still alive with flavor after a century. Dr. Benjamin Ichinose has found thirty-year-old white burgundies that were still perfect to drink.

The quality and length of the cork are important factors in the aging of wines. I have in my cellar some California reds, with ordinary corks, that are more than fifty years old. I keep them mainly to show my students what spoiled wines are like. While most of these bottles that I have opened (with great difficulty because the

191

corks fell apart) have been faintly acetic, they all were still drinkable, and I occasionally have found a bottle with a better cork, that was really a pleasure to drink.

There is no way to predict wines' longevity except by experience with the wines of individual vineyards, and this, too, is often unreliable. For example, André Tchelistcheff, the former winemaker at Beaulieu, tells me that his 1946 Private Reserve Cabernet Sauvignon, pronounced great when it was young, was tired by age nine, but that his 1951 vintage was still alive with much of its youthful quality in 1974.

As old wines deposit sediment and corks grow soft, some owners of cellars decant them off the sediment and recork them after twenty years or so. This also calls for refilling, from another bottle, the headspace created by evaporation. Dr. Ichinose, who has the most extensive cellar in my part of the country, has conducted research on this point and has been advised that recorking is likely to hasten an old wine's demise. (Incidentally, Dr. Ichinose keeps his cellar air-conditioned at 47° for champagnes, 55° for whites, and 58° for reds. He also uses a hygrometer to watch the humidity, which he keeps well above fifty percent.)

Many of my friends have cellar books to keep records of their aging wines. They record such things as the source of each wine, its price, the quantity purchased, when it is used, with whom as guests and with what foods, the quantity left, and where in the cellar the bottles are stored. I have never had the time to do this, but if I ever do, I plan to use a card file rather than the handsome cellar books I have received as gifts.

My cellar contains far too many different wines from different vineyards and countries to fit in any of the present cellar books.

THE PROFIT FROM YOUR CELLAR

How about wines as an investment for profit? The quick answer is that it is illegal to sell wine or any other alcoholic beverage without first obtaining federal and state permits or licenses. (Temporary licenses are granted for those annual wine auctions you read about.) This does not stop some of my friends from buying wines from one another or from cellars left but forgotten by estates. I am told that it is possible (in some states) for an estate to get a special one-time license to sell the contents of a cellar. My view is that connoisseurs who are growing old should drink up or otherwise dispose of their finest wines, which may be too fine to be appreciated by their heirs.

Some retailing importers sell futures on the latest vintages of the finer European wines. Buying futures means buying unseen a wine that is still in the cask, to be delivered when bottled two or three years later. You pay a lower price now than you would pay later, but you pay it in full now, and you still have to bottle-age the wine after it is delivered. I have also heard of occasional offers of futures in California wines, but mainly by vintners who happened to be short of cash.

It seems to me that the real profits in your wine cellar are in your pleasure in watching your wines improve, in the opportunity to drink wines of superbly

193

aged quality which scarcity has made astronomically expensive, and in paying a guest the high compliment of taking him to the cellar with the privilege of choosing the wine to be served at dinner. Your greatest reward of all, however, is in observing the wonder of how wines mellow, of how they reveal new layers of flavor and character, like old friends.

15 / Is Wine for You?

It would be well to begin this chapter by stating that you should *not* drink wine or any other alcoholic beverage if: (a) you have a peptic ulcer; (b) you suffer from a chronic kidney ailment, pancreatitis, or liver disease; (c) you have taken a tranquilizer pill, which in this combination can tranquilize you much more than you would like, or (d) you have religious scruples against the use of all such drinks.

The latter interdiction is based on the tragic demonstration furnished during the Prohibition era that any form of prohibition leads to excessive consumption. However, I get a certain impious satisfaction from the vast volume of alcoholic tonics (including many that have wine as their base) consumed in this country by religious teetotalers, who find the daily use of these nostrums gives them a feeling of well-being.

There also is something weird in the paradox of certain church groups who interpret Scripture as requiring total abstention, while other denominations find, in the same Holy Bible, clear commands to use wine in their most sacred rites of worship. I perceive something grimly comical in the dozens of volumes that have been penned by fanatics in attempts to prove that the recommendations of wine in the Old and New Testaments meant only unfermented grape juice. Anyone who has ever heard of *Saccharoymces ellipsoideus* (wine yeasts) knows that unless the Apostles were familiar with either pasteurization, refrigeration, or sulfur dioxide, the grape juice of the Bible would inevitably have turned into wine.

The drunkenness common among Moslems, whose religion commands them to abstain from wine, is another demonstration that a feeling of guilt produces excesses. In most northern countries, including many parts of the United States, a kind of mass guilt complex still surrounds the use of all alcoholic beverages. But among the Latin nations wine seems specifically excluded from classification with intoxicating liquor. Ask an Italian: "Do you drink?" and he may answer in the negative, because he uses only wine.

Returning to the medical aspects, doctors are now coming to know a good deal about wine's values that they did not know a generation ago. Strangely enough, earlier physicians were aware of the very things that modern science has only lately rediscovered.

Medical history furnishes the explanation of this. For centuries—since the time of Hippocrates, the father of medicine—doctors have observed the beneficial effects of wine upon individuals both in sickness and in health. Its prescription was virtually universal. Then came the modern era of experimental medicine, in which every pharmaceutical substance has had to be tested and to prove its values. Wine, the oldest of medicines, was not among those first subjected to such tests; and as a result, its medicinal use gradually declined. With the advent of Prohibition in 1920, the many references to wine in the United States Pharmacopoeia were summarily dropped. Thus an entire generation of doctors began practicing their profession with virtually no knowledge of wine.

In more recent years, however, comprehensive programs of wine research have been carried on in many university laboratories and clinics. The findings were good news to doctors: that wines are the most effective natural liquid stimulants of appetite; that wine can aid in the prevention or treatment of arteriosclerosis; that it may be effective in reducing the severity of attacks of angina pectoris or even in preventing them altogether, and that *dry* wines have value in the treatment of diabetes.

Specialists in geriatrics are learning that the ancient Greek physician Galen was right when he called wine "the nurse of old age." Now nursing homes are beginning to serve their patients a daily choice of wines. Many hospitals, too, with physicians' approval, are adding table wines to convalescing patients' lunch and evening meal trays. The principal values observed are the promotion of appetite and euphoria. The latter means fewer complaints from patients and consequently more rest for the doctor and the nurse.

A number of physicians of my acquaintance now

include wine in reducing diets for the obese. They cite American and Italian studies that show wine calories can replace carbohydrate calories and that patients tend to decrease their carbohydrate intake as they increase their intake of wine. The internist who once guided me in a successful sixty-pound weight-reduction program allowed me my normal daily quarter-bottle of dry table wine.

(Typical red, rosé, and white table wines contain from 22 to 26 calories per fluid ounce and sherries 38 to 45, depending on their alcoholic content and on whether they are dry or sweet; and sweet dessert wines from 45 to 48. Four ounces of 12 percent dry red wine contribute fewer calories (96.4) than two slices of bread (110). A standard six-ounce serving of chablis delivers a fifth fewer calories (132) than a standard eight-ounce glass of milk with 166.)

I have never forgotten the comment of a certain vintner when, some years ago, I showed him the report by Dr. A. L. Soresi of New York that certain wines had been found to have values in the sedation of post-operative cases—when the wines were administered rectally. "For that purpose," my winemaker friend remarked, "I recommend the wine of my principal competitor!"

Researchers exploring the physiological effects of drinks can now tell us with a fair degree of certainty what happens when wine gets past our lips. You do not feel the effect of alcohol until it first passes through the walls of your stomach or of your small intestine into your bloodstream, then reaches your heart and is pumped through the body, where it attacks the fatty nerve tissues, especially those of the brain. But if you have food in your stomach, it delays the passage of alcohol into the bloodstream and makes it gradual. This is one of the reasons why wine, whose principal use is with meals, is less intoxicating, more temperate than other drinks. It also confirms the rule, long known to those who must attend cocktail parties for business reasons, that one way to drink and remain sober is first to line your stomach with a fatty substance such as cream or olive oil, or with high-protein snacks such as meat tidbits or nuts.

Wine does not stimulate, as has long been imagined; the alcohol it naturally contains relaxes you instead. It gives you a warm feeling; it expands your blood vessels, sends warm blood into the small capillaries of your skin. (This explains why some habitual topers develop red noses: the surface blood vessels have been distended so constantly that they remain so.)

On the other hand, some people cannot drink wine; they may be allergic to some substance in grapes. Others are sensitive only to certain red wines that are high in histamine content. And alcoholics and potential alcoholics should never drink wine or alcohol in any other form.

This raises the question of why, among the drunkards populating the skid rows of some American cities, there is the miserable human specimen called a "wino" (a word that makes every vintner gag). There are police officials who associate the "wino's" sickness with the wine he consumes. Medical authorities have had dif-

199

ficulty convincing policemen of the rather simple truth: This type of skid row inhabitant is a chronic alcoholic who cannot afford the price of heavily taxed liquor. Wine is inexpensive—so he gets his alcohol from wine. These individuals do not even like the taste of wine; they buy stronger beverages whenever they can. Medical studies of their histories show that most of them became alcoholics before they began drinking wine. Their sickness is due not to the alcohol they consume but to the proteins and vitamins they don't. They suffer from malnutrition.

Massive evidence assembled in many countries (France, Italy, Brazil, New York, California) in recent years confirms a further fact—long apparent to anyone who has observed wine drinking in Latin countries— that the regular mealtime use of this beverage serves as a preventive of alcoholism. Dr. William Dock of New York expresses it this way: "Abuse of alcohol is rare in those who come from the lands of the olive and the vine, where children see and participate in moderate wine drinking at mealtime, now as they have done for many centuries."

In families where wine is the common beverage, children are given wine diluted with water, and drunkenness is looked upon with no less disgust than any other kind of animal misbehavior. Among cultured Italians, even a single instance of being intoxicated would cause an individual to be ostracized from polite society.

There is nothing new in the observation that wine is a temperate beverage; it was known long before

Thomas Jefferson wrote: "No nation is drunken where wine is cheap, and none sober where the dearness of wine substitutes ardent spirits as the common beverage." All that is new is the measured scientific proof.

America is maturing as a nation and in its appreciation of the finer things of life. One of the signs of this maturity is the growing appreciation of the civilized beverage, wine.

Acknowledgments

Hundreds of my friends among winegrowers, enologists, research workers, wine merchants, and fellow oenophiles have contributed during the past forty years to the information contained in this book. In expressing my appreciation, however, I should make it clear that none of them is in any way responsible for my errors or for my contradictions of vintners' advertising and of the industry's romantic wine lore. No industry member has read any part of the manuscript.

In my attempt to condense the essential facts about the wines of many countries, I have reviewed and found invaluable guidance in the many excellent articles and books by such noted authorities as Maynard Amerine, Harold Berg, the late William V. Cruess, Maynard Joslyn, Edouard Kressmann, Chauncey Leake, Alexis Lichine, Salvatore Lucia, Harold Olmo, Cyril Ray, Frank Schoonmaker, Vernon Singleton, Philip Wagner, A. Dinsmoor Webb, and Albert J. Winkler. My suggestions for further reading include the outstanding books by some of these authors.

I am especially indebted to the great enologists, Julius Fessler and André Tchelistcheff, for trying to answer my most difficult questions about how to determine the aging potential of wines; to Karl Petrowsky, editor of *The International Wine Letter and Digest*, for his help in indicating the relative dryness or sweetness of the principal German wines; to Benjamin Ichinose for furnishing me the results of his long experience and extensive research on the planning of wine cellars, and to Ernest G. Mittelberger, director of the Wine Museum of San Francisco, for suggesting several of the topics newly covered in this edition.

Warm personal thanks are also due Peter M.F. Sichel for his precise translation of the 1971 German Wine Law; home economist and wineglass authority Marjorie Lumm for her assistance with the chapter on wine cookery, and Mabel Bolton and Steven Edmunds for patiently reading and criticizing the principal chapters from their standpoint as knowledgeable retail wine merchants.

Finally, I wish to express my thanks to my wife Eleanor for her precise editing and typing of the manuscript, and to my daughter Susan for her evenings spent patiently helping me compile the Index.

Glossary of Some Common Wine Terms

See the Index for additional terms and explanations

Abboccato, Abocado   Italian and Spanish for semi-sweet.

Acidity   Tartness, the sharp taste of natural fruit acids.

Amabile (ah-*mah*-be-lay)   Italian for sweet.

Amaro (ah-*ma*-ro)   Italian for bitter, but also used to mean very dry.

Amelioration   Addition of sugar (chaptalization) or water (to reduce acidity of grapes), permissible in the United States if the volume of the finished wine is not increased more than 35 percent, but prohibited in California for grape wine.

Amontillado   Flavorful, full-bodied type of Spanish sherry, usually dry.

Amoroso   Medium-sweet type of Spanish sherry.

Ampelography   The study of grape varieties, or a book of vine varieties.

Appellation contrôlée   French label term meaning that a wine was grown and made in the legally delimited district whose name it bears, from approved grape varieties only, and according to the locally recognized method of winemaking.

A.O.C.   Abbreviation for Appellation d'Origine Contrôlée.

Argols   The crystalline deposit of natural tartrates in wine vats, sometimes also found in bottles or adhering to corks.

Aroma   Fragrance of fresh grapes, as distinguished from bouquet.

Astringency   Puckery quality caused by tannin from the skins and seeds of grapes; lessens as wine matures.

Aus Eigenem Lesegut (ows *eye*-gen-em *lay*-zeh-goot)   German label term meaning estate-bottled.

Auslese (*ows*-lay-zeh)   German for a wine made from selected ripe grapes; indicates the wine is semidry to semisweet.

Balanced   Said of a wine in which acidity, sweetness, and flavor are in pleasing proportions.

Barrique (bah-reek)   The 225-liter (60-gallon) barrel used in Bordeaux.

Beerenauslese   German for wine made from selected fully ripe grapes; always sweet.

Bereich (bay-*reich*)   German label term used to modify a famous vineyard name, means the wine was only grown in the same district.

Bianco (bee-*ahn*-co)   Italian for white.

205

Big   Said of a wine of extra body, flavor, and alcoholic content.

Blanc, Blanco, Branco   French, Spanish, Portuguese for white.

Blanc de Blancs (blahn-duh-blahn)   "White of whites," meaning a white wine made of white grapes, such as champagne made of Chardonnay. Also used as the names of some wineries' special blends of still white wines, ranging from dry to medium-dry.

Bodega (bo-*day*-ga)   Spanish for winery.

Body   Substance or texture of a wine, opposite of thinness.

Bonded winery   An establishment where wines are made and stored under bond to guarantee payment of the federal excise tax.

Bottled at the Winery   Means the wine was bottled at the winery where it was "produced," which *see.*

Bottle ripe   Said of a wine sufficiently aged in cask to be bottled.

Bottle sickness   Unbalance of wine flavor after bottling or after rough travel, caused by excessive aeration; clears up when wine is allowed to rest one to several weeks.

Bouquet   Winy fragrance as distinguished from aroma.

Brix   A scale of sweetness based on specific gravity of wine or juice, measured by hydrometer; also called Balling.

Brut   French term for almost-dry champagnes.

Bulk process   Label term for champagne made by the Charmat or closed-cuvée method.

Butt   The 130-gallon cask in which Spanish sherry is traditionally exported.

Capsule   The foil or plastic covering for the mouth and neck of a wine bottle to protect the closure.

Carafe wine   Young, inexpensive wine served by the carafe in a restaurant, usually called the "house wine."

Carbonic maceration   Old, newly popular wine-making method by which tanks are filled with whole grapes including stems, and fermentation without oxygen occurs spontaneously in the intact grapes with the release of carbon dioxide.

Cépage (say-pahzh)   French term for grape variety.

Chaptalization   Addition of sugar to grape juice before fermentation, practiced in areas and seasons where grapes lack sufficient natural sugar content to produce wines of standard alcoholic strength.

Château   A winegrowing estate.

Château sauterne   "Château" followed by a winery's name is usually its proprietary name for its sweet sauterne.

Clean   Said of a wine fresh on the palate and free of any off-taste.

Clone   In grape nomenclature, a variation, subvariety, or strain that has developed within a given grape variety; for example, the more than

207

200 clones of Pinot Noir.

Clos (clo)   French term for an enclosed or a once-enclosed or walled vineyard.

Cloying   Said of wines, usually sweet, that satiate the taste.

Cooperage   Wine vats or tanks, a term derived from cooper, one who makes or repairs barrels.

Corked, corky   Musty odor or taste in wine caused by a moldy cork.

Crackling   Slightly sparkling, less so than champagne.

Crémant (kray-mahn)   French term for semi-sparkling wine, usually more effervescent than crackling but less so than champagne.

Cru (crew)   Literally, in French, a growth or tract of land such as a vineyard, but principally means a vineyard's rank in the 1855 classification or ranking of Bordeaux vineyards and their wines into five classes or crus. Eighty-three Médoc, Graves, and Sauternes châteaux were classified in 1855, but since then hundreds more have classified themselves as first to fifth crus or as crus *exceptionnels* or as crus *bourgeois.*

Cuvée (cew-vay)   A batch or blend of wine, such as to make champagne, or to be marketed under a particular name.

Demijohn   The 4.9-gallon, usually wicker-covered, wine jug.

Demi-sec   French for semi-sweet, but usually means fully sweet.

Dessert wine   U.S. legal term for wines over 14

percent and not over 21 percent in alcoholic strength by volume; includes appetizer wines such as sherries.

Dinner wine   Table wine.

D.O.C.   Abbreviation on Italian labels for *Denominazione di Origine Controllata.*

Doce, Dolce, Dulce   Sweet in Portuguese, Italian, Spanish.

Dry   Literally means without sugar, the opposite of sweet, but often used for medium-dry and even medium-sweet wines.

Domaine   A winegrowing estate.

Earthy   Said of a wine of coarse taste suggestive of earth.

Eiswein (*ice*-vine)   German term for wine made from frozen grapes; always sweet.

Enology   The science and study of winemaking.

Erzeuger Abfüllung (er-*tsoy*-ger *ahb*-few-lung)   German label term meaning bottled at the winery.

Espumoso, Espumante   Spanish and Portuguese for sparkling like champagne.

Estate-Bottled   Originally meant wine bottled at the winery adjoining the proprietor's vineyard, but interpretations have broadened it to include wines from vineyards in the same county, related to the winery.

Fiasco   The Italian straw-covered flask primarily associated with chianti.

Fining   Clarification of wine by adding substances such as egg white, which settle to the bottom of the container, carrying with them grape substances that were held in suspension.

Fino   Very dry, pale, flor-flavor type of Spanish sherry.

Flat   Lacking in acidity, dull, uninteresting.

Flinty   Said of extremely dry white wines, such as French chablis, whose bouquet is reminiscent of flint struck against steel.

Flor   Flavor produced in sherry by a special yeast that forms a film on the surface of wine; differs from the oxidized or madeirized sherry flavor.

Fortified   Said of a wine to which wine spirit (brandy) has been added, port and sherry for example.

Foxy   The familiar "grape flavor" of fresh grape juice and grape jelly. Its source is mainly an ester, methyl anthranilate, contained in such native American grape varieties as Catawba, Concord, Delaware.

Frizzante (free-*zahn*-tay)   Italian for crackling or pétillant.

Fruity   Said of wine with pronounced aroma and taste of fresh, ripe grapes; often but not necessarily sweet.

Gassy   Containing excess carbon-dioxide from incomplete fermentation, or re-fermentation.

Generic   Term used for wine type-names of geographic origin which have acquired general or worldwide meaning and use, such as burgundy, chablis, champagne, port, sherry.

Green   Said of a wine with excessive fruit acidity,

210

especially if it has a malic (apple-like) aroma.

Harsh   Excessively tart or astringent to an unpleasant degree.

Haut (oh)   French term meaning high or upper in relation to the Médoc district of Bordeaux, also used to designate some sweet sauternes.

Headspace   The air-space between a wine and its closure.

Heady   Said of wines unusually high in alcoholic strength.

House wine   A wine selected and featured by a restaurant, usually but not always served in carafes or by the glass.

Hybrid   A grape variety created by crossing two or more varieties. Refers primarily to crosses by French hybridizers between Vinifera and American wild vines to obtain immunity of the latter against the phylloxera vine pest. French hybrids, because they do not require grafting to phylloxera-resistant roots, are also called direct-producers.

Jeroboam   Extra-large bottle, holds four to six normal bottles.

Kabinett   German label term for wine from a limited area, made without chaptalization, usually dry.

Labrusca   The native American "foxy" family of grapes, exemplified by Catawba, Concord, Delaware, Dutchess, Elvira, Ives; not related to the Lambrusco grape and wine of Italy.

211

Late harvest   Wine made from late-harvested grapes, usually extra-sweet and alcoholic.

Lees   The sediment deposited by wine during fermentation and aging in cask.

Light   Opposite of full-bodied. Also, legally, not over 14 percent in alcoholic content by volume.

Limousin (lee-moo-zan)   Refers to casks of oak from Limoges in France, but generally misused to designate any barrel of European oak.

Madeirized   Oxidized, baked, such as by the heating method practiced in Madeira.

Magnum   Double-size bottle.

Malic   Apple-like aroma of malic acid from incompletely ripened grapes.

Malolactic fermentation   Secondary fermentation in which lactic acid bacteria convert malic acid in wine into lactic acid, reducing the total acidity and releasing carbon dioxide. It improves many red wines and adds complexity to their flavors. If it occurs in the bottle it may cause gassiness, such as in the vinho verde wines of Portugal, but may also cause a wine to be temporarily turbid and unpalatable.

Mellow   Soft, mature, ripe, but also used on dessert wines as a euphemism for sweet.

Méthode champenoise   (may-tode-chahm-pen-wahs) Term for the bottle-fermentation method of making champagne, including disgorging by hand.

Monopole   Means a proprietary wine name owned exclusively by a bottler or négociant and used to distinguish a particular wine blend.

Mousseux (moo-suh)   French for sparkling like champagne.

Muscadine   The Rotundifolia family of native American grapes found in the southeastern states, of which the best-known variety is the Scuppernong.

Must   Crushed grapes or juice before fermentation.

Musty   Unpleasant odor or flavor of moldy casks or moldy corks.

Natural, naturel   Designates champagnes that contain no sweetening dosage, completely dry.

Natural pure flavors   Label term used on such flavored ("special natural") wines as sangría and the "pop" types, meaning the added flavors are natural, such as fruit juices, herbs, extracts, etc.

Nebuchadnezzar   Giant wine bottle, holds twenty normal bottles.

Négociant (nay-go-syahn)   French for a wholesale wine merchant, blender, and shipper. Some négociants are also producers of wine.

Neutral   Said of wines lacking in flavor.

Nose   Wine taster's term for aroma or bouquet.

Nutty   Oxidized or sherry-like flavor reminiscent of walnuts; madeirized; *rancio* in Spanish.

Oaky   Flavors imparted by aging of wine in oak casks, different between American white oak and European oak varieties.

Ordinaire   French for young wine of everyday quality.

Oxidized   Sherry-like or madeirized flavor caused

by action of oxygen on wine, due mainly to exposure to air, heat, or light.

Passe-tout-grains (pahs-too-gran)   French red burgundy made from a blend of Gamay and Pinot Noir grapes.

Passito (pah-*see*-to)   Italian for sweet from semidried grapes.

Pasteurization   Brief heating to prevent or arrest fermentation.

Pétillant (pay-tee-yahn)   French term for crackling or slightly sparkling wine.

Pièce (pee-*ess*)   The 56- to 60-gallon barrel used in Burgundy.

Pipe   The 320-liter (115 gallons) cask traditionally used for Portuguese port.

Piquant   Pleasantly tart.

Pomace   The residue of grape solids after fermentation and pressing, *marc* in French.

Pourriture noble (poo-ree-tyur-*no*-bl)   French for the botrytis cinerea mold, literally "noble rot," Edelfäule in German, which dehydrates grapes left late on the vine and concentrates their juice.

Proprietary   Said of a wine type-name owned exclusively by the winery or the bottler.

Qualitätswein (kval-ee-*tats*-vine)   German label term for wines above Tafelwein quality, including chaptalized wines. Qualitätswein mit Prädikat means wine not chaptalized and with special attributes, such as Kabinett, Spätlese, Auslese, and Eiswein.

Racking   Drawing wine from a cask in which it has

deposited sediment, into a fresh container.

Raisiny   Flavor or aroma suggesting raisins.

Reserva, riserva   Spanish and Italian for wines aged in cask.

Rosado, Rosato   Spanish, Portuguese, Italian for rosé, pink.

Rosso   Italian for red.

Rotundifolia   The Muscadine native grape species of the southeastern states, such as Scuppernong.

Rouge   French for red.

Rounded   Said of a wine harmoniously balanced in body and flavor.

Salmanazar   Extra-large wine bottle, contains twelve normal bottles.

Scuppernong   Best known of the Muscadine family of native American grapes that grow in the southeastern states.

Sec   French for "dry"; secco in Italian, seco in Portuguese, Spanish.

Sekt   German term for champagne and other effervescent wines, derived from French sec.

Soft   Said of a wine low in astringency.

Solera   A series of casks in which wines are periodically blended, young wines with old.

Sour   Aroma and taste of acetic acid; vinegary; said of partially-spoiled wine.

Spätlese (*shpate*-lay-zuh)   German term for wine made of late-picked grapes and not chaptalized.

Spicy   Said of wines with pronounced varietal aroma and taste, Gewürztraminer for example.

Split   The quarter-bottle, 6.4 ounces, soon to become 3/16th liter (6.3 ounces).

Spumante (spoo-*mahn*-tay)   Italian for sparkling like champagne.

Stemmy   Unpleasant aroma of wine fermented with grape stems.

Sulfur   Generally refers to sulfur dioxide, traditionally added to wine to inhibit fermentation or re-fermentation; sometimes too apparent in a finished wine.

Tafelwein (*tahf*-el-vine)   German label term for wine of less than Kabinett quality.

Tannin   Astringent natural substance derived from skins and seeds of grapes and from oak containers; essential for wines to improve with age. Tannin content lessens as wines mature.

Tart   Agreeably sharp in taste, from the natural fruit acids in wine.

Tawny   Brownish-red color of some ports, said to result from age.

Tinto   Spanish for red.

Trockenbeerenauslese   German for wine from grapes left on the vine to ripen until virtually dry, then individually selected to make a very sweet, enormously expensive wine.

Varietal   Said of wine having the pronounced aroma and flavor of a grape variety; also the general term for wines labeled with names of grape varieties, and misused to refer to grape varieties whose names often appear on labels of "varietal" wines.

Vin du pays (van-dew-pay)   French for wine of the country, usually means young wine sold in the locality where it is grown.

Viniculture   Science or study of grape production for wine and of the making of wine.

Vinifera (vy-*nif*-er-a)   Family name of the Old World wine-grape species, from the hundreds of members of which the world's best and principal wines are made.

Vino corriente   Spanish for young wine of everyday quality, equivalent to French vin ordinaire.

Vinous (*vy*-nus)   Having a winy flavor, as distinguished from fruity.

V.D.Q.S.   Abbreviation for *Vins Délimités de Qualité Supérieur,* a French geographic classification similar to but less restrictive than Appellation Contrôlée.

Vintage   The harvesting of grapes and the making of wine; also, the wine produced in that year. A season of unusually favorable weather is called a "vintage year" and is said to produce "vintage wines."

Vintner   Translated as wine merchant, generally used for wine producers and winery proprietors as well.

Viticulture   The cultivation, science, and study of grapes.

Wine   The fermented juice of sound, ripe grapes without addition or abstraction except as may occur in governmentally authorized cellar

217

treatment. Other fermented beverages may be called wine with appropriate qualification, but "wine" without qualification means only the fermented juice of grapes.

Wineglass   Any glass especially used for wine, but strangely defined in dictionaries, perhaps from outdated medical usage, as holding only two fluid ounces.

Winery   A place where wine is produced or processed.

Woody   Said of wine with excessive odor or taste of wood.

Yeasty   The odor of yeast in young wines before racking, often evident in some young wines after bottling.

Suggested for Further Reading

available in paperback editions

Adams, Leon D., *The Wines of America.* Boston: San Francisco Book Company/Houghton Mifflin Company, 1975.*

Amerine, M.A., and Singleton, V.L., *Wine: An Introduction for Americans.* Berkeley: University of California Press, 1965.*

Bespaloff, Alexis, *Wine: A Complete Introduction.* New York: The New American Library, Inc., Signet Books, 1971.*

Chroman, Nathan, *The Treasury of American Wines.* New York: Ridge Press/Crown Publishers, Inc., 1973.

Evans, Len, *Australia and New Zealand Complete Book of Wine.* Sydney: Paul Hamlyn Pty. Ltd., 1973.

Fluchère, Henri, *Wines.* New York: Western Publishing Company, Inc., Golden Press, 1973.*

Jacquelin, Louis, and Poulain, René, *The Wines and Vineyards of France,* rev. ed. Translated by T.A. Layton. London: Paul Hamlyn Ltd., 1965.

Johnson, Hugh, *Wine.* New York: Simon and Schuster, 1966.

Lichine, Alexis, *New Encyclopedia of Wines and Spirits,* 2nd ed., rev. New York: Alfred A. Knopf, Inc., 1974.

219

Lichine, Alexis, *The Wines of France,* 5th ed., rev. New York: Alfred A. Knopf, Inc., 1969.

Lucia, S.P., *A History of Wine as Therapy.* Philadelphia: J.B. Lippincott Company, 1963.

Massee, William E., *Massee's Wine Handbook,* rev. ed. New York: Doubleday and Company, Inc., 1971.

Melville, John, and Morgan, Jefferson, *Guide to California Wines,* 4th ed., rev. New York: E.P. Dutton and Company, Inc., 1973.*

Ray, Cyril, *The Wines of Italy.* New York: McGraw-Hill Book Company, 1966.

Read, Jan, *The Wines of Spain and Portugal.* New York: Hippocrene Books, Inc., 1974.

Schoonmaker, Frank, *Encyclopedia of Wine,* 5th ed., rev. New York: Hastings House, Publishers, Inc., 1973.

Wagner, Philip M., *American Wines and Winemaking,* 5th ed. New York: Alfred A. Knopf, Inc., 1974.

Wildman, Frederick S., Jr., *A Wine Tour of France.* New York: William Morrow and Company, Inc., 1972.

Index

225

Commonsense Book of Wine